RELIGION AND SCIENCE
THE BASICS

Religion and science are arguably the two most powerful social forces in the world today; however, they are widely perceived to be in irreconcilable conflict. This unique book provides an introduction to the crucial ongoing questions and arguments in this controversial field.

Examining critical arguments through thematic debates, the author, renowned expert Philip Clayton, presents a balanced response to essential issues including:

- science *or* religion, or science *and* religion?
- Intelligent Design vs. the New Atheists
- the role of scientific and religious ethics – designer drugs, AI, and stem cell research
- the future of science and the future of religion.

Viewpoints from a range of world religions and different scientific disciplines are explored, making this book essential reading for all those wishing to formulate their own questions and opinions about this much debated subject.

Philip Clayton is Ingraham Professor and Dean of Claremont School of Theology, and Provost of Claremont Lincoln University USA. Author or editor of some twenty books, he is widely recognized internationally as a leading figure in the field of religion and science.

The Basics

RELIGION AND SCIENCE

THE BASICS

Philip Clayton

Routledge
Taylor & Francis Group

LONDON AND NEW YORK

First published 2012
by Routledge
2 Park Square, Milton Park, Abingdon, Oxon OX14 4RN

Simultaneously published in the USA and Canada
by Routledge
711 Third Avenue, New York, NY 10017

Routledge is an imprint of the Taylor & Francis Group, an informa business

British Library Cataloguing in Publication Data
A catalogue record for this book is available from the British Library

Library of Congress Cataloging in Publication Data
Clayton, Philip, 1956–
  Religion and science: the basics/Philip Clayton.
  p. cm. – (The basics)
  Includes bibliographical references.
  1. Religion and science. I. Title.
  BL240.3.C54 2012
  201'.65–dc22

                                                                2011009500

ISBN: 978-0-415-59855-2 (hbk)
ISBN: 978-0-415-59856-9 (pbk)
ISBN: 978-0-203-80444-5 (ebk)

Typeset in Bembo
by Wearset Ltd, Boldon, Tyne and Wear

MIX
Paper from
responsible sources
FSC www.fsc.org FSC® C004839

Printed and bound in Great Britain by
TJ International Ltd, Padstow, Cornwall

CONTENTS

PREFACE

Like many philosophical questions, the questions that arise at the boundaries between the sciences and the religions will likely be with us for as long as there are humans to ask questions. Unlike some philosophical disputes, however, this debate is of immense practical importance. Science and religion may just be the two most powerful social forces in the world today (money comes in a close third). All of us have a stake in whether they engage in a war to the death or become partners for the good of society and the planet.

Many different interests might lead one to explore the possible relationships between religion and science. They fall roughly into three groups:

1 Religious:

- You are a religious person who wants to show that your religious beliefs are consistent with today's science.
- You are a religious person who has concluded that your beliefs clash with science, and you want to be able to convince people that they should side with you and against science.
- You are a religious person who concludes that your beliefs clash with science, yet you don't want to make affirmations that undercut science. So you are trying to determine what (if anything) you can salvage from your former belief system.

2 Science:

- You are a scientist who believes that religion is deeply destructive to the quest for scientific knowledge, and you want to learn enough about it so that you can demolish it more effectively.

- You are a scientifically inclined person who wants to find out whether religion is an opponent to science, a friend, or neutral to the scientific quest.
- You are a scientist and also deeply religious, and you are encouraged by the many compatibilities that you find between scientific knowledge and your own religious faith.

3 Other:

- You are neither scientist nor religious, but you believe that both are important social forces in today's world. You want to study the field to know whether or not there is an intrinsic conflict between these two powerful forces in the contemporary world, in order to make up your mind about what you should believe and do.
- You are interested in the topic for purely intellectual reasons. You find that it raises some fascinating philosophical questions, and you like to reflect on and debate about these issues.
- You believe that the battle between science and religion is unnecessary, even harmful, and you wish to find ways to decrease the antagonism between the two camps.
- You believe there are potential partnerships between science and religion and you want to find ways in which the two might work together more productively.

These ten reasons are only a starter; you can extend the list at will.

In short, there turns out to be a great variety of ways to relate science and religion, and people bring vastly different interests to the debate. Some are deeply committed to scientific practice and the success of science; they believe that scientific knowledge is crucial for humanity to survive and to answer the challenges that we face today. Some believe that science provides all the guidelines humans need for making fundamental ethical and political decisions, and that it (rather than religion or philosophy) should determine our view of the world. Some are deeply committed to a specific religious tradition, or to spiritual perspectives more generally, or are seeking to make up their minds about religious claims. Many bring *both* religious and scientific interests to the debate.

Some come to the debate primarily wanting to know what is true. Others are far more skeptical about ever being able to resolve the truth questions; in their view, practical or pragmatic issues are far more urgent. The former group might look for an integration of science and religion as providing the truest picture of the way reality actually is. The latter group has less to say about that question; its members are looking for partnerships where science and religion can work in a complementary fashion to address the planet's most pressing issues.

This book will not tell you what to believe about these issues. It is organized instead *around the questions themselves*, in the conviction that each person must come to answers for himself or herself. Clearly I believe that the questions themselves are extremely important, whether for their practical significance, or for the ways in which they may guide us toward true answers, or for both reasons. (If I didn't believe this, I wouldn't have written the book.) Great questions are cheapened by easy answers. They require the discipline of listening, reflecting, and suspending judgment for a time. One needs to learn to 'sit with the questions,' as my Buddhist friends often say.

The pages before you are intended as a first introduction to this fascinating field. Those with more advanced knowledge of some part of the debate may still find it helpful to get an overview of what the discipline as a whole looks like. Those with no background at all in the sciences may find a few of the sections in Chapters 4 to 6 a bit of a stretch. But the sciences are important enough that they are worth the attention. Grasp what you can of the core concepts and let the rest go; you will quickly see how important they are for understanding the religious responses. Those interested in going deeper are encouraged to move on to the *Oxford Handbook of Religion and Science* and to other sources cited throughout the text.

Perhaps I should disclose one authorial prejudice here, before we get started. People often tell me, 'It's just not possible to have a reasonable discussion about religion and science.' I have to acknowledge that numerous web pages, newspaper articles, and TV shows will offer you irrational, irate, even angry treatments of the subject. (Public statements by certain well-known scientists and religious leaders don't help matters much either.) This book is written in the belief that the failure to have civil discussions of these topics is not the inevitable outcome. If you declare reason

'DOA' (dead on arrival), it's not likely to be able to help you much. Indeed, people often use such skepticism as their personal license to say and do the most unreasonable things. By contrast, if you attempt to formulate a reasonable position and marshal the best arguments you can find in its defense, you may be surprised at how far you can get. This book is dedicated to all those who are willing to make the effort.

Special thanks are due to my research assistant at Claremont, Justin Heinzekehr, who prepared the index, helped with multiple references and with fact checking, and in general managed the revision process; to the three readers for Routledge, whose requests for changes received the closest of attention (and not just because the press wouldn't have published otherwise!); and to Jheri Cravens, who once again produced a faultless typescript in record time and at crazy hours. I dedicate this book to the many scientists over the past two decades who have engaged with me in open-ended reflection about the broader implications of the best science of our day, and to the religious persons who have had the courage to challenge their own communities to wrestle more deeply with scientific knowledge and the spirit of scientific inquiry. These two groups are the unsung heroes of the future of religion and, I dare say, of the future of science as well.

THE BASIC QUESTION
SCIENCE *OR* RELIGION, OR SCIENCE *AND* RELIGION?

THE DEBATE THAT NO ONE CAN AVOID

It is hard to imagine any institutions in human culture and existence today with deeper roots than religion and science. Religion is so basic to human history that the human species has been called *homo religiosus*, the religious animal. Indeed, some scholars even connect the origins of our species, *Homo sapiens sapiens*, to the first archeological signs of religious rituals and practices. A huge proportion of the world's population today is identified with at least one of the major religious traditions of the world.

It is equally impossible to imagine humanity without science. By 1900, about three centuries after the dawn of modern science, it was clear that this new means of studying the natural world and organizing our beliefs about it was transforming humanity more than perhaps any other development in the history of our species. By the end of World War II, when much of Europe had been reduced to rubble and Hiroshima to an atomic fall-out zone, science had changed the face of the planet for ever. Today there is virtually no aspect of human existence that does not depend in some way upon scientific results and technological inventions. From immunizations to heart surgery, from fertilizer to genetically modified crops, from our cell phones to our computers, from roads to airplanes, from the bananas on our table to our 'cash' in the bank, existence without science has become inconceivable.

As we will see in the following pages, the impact of science is not only limited to its products. The scientific mindset has transformed humanity's views of what knowledge is, how it is obtained, and how knowledge claims are evaluated. Even people whose central moral and religious beliefs are not determined by science are still impacted by the growth of science, since *others* will judge their knowledge claims in light of their agreement with or divergence from scientific results.

Science and religion: compatibility or conflict? Should we talk about 'science and religion,' or should it be 'science *versus* religion'? By the time you finish this book, you will have a good sense of the whole range of answers that have been given to this question and the best arguments that are being made on both sides. This should give you enough information to make up your own mind and to defend your own positions in each of the major areas of the debate.

Certainly the dominant message in our culture today is that science and religion stand in deep tension. Nowhere is this message clearer than in the debate between naturalism and theism. *Naturalism* is the view that all that exists are natural objects within the universe – the combinations of physical mass and energy that make up planets and stars, oceans and mountains, microbes and humans. In normal usage, naturalism usually implies the claim that real knowledge of these natural objects comes through, or is at least controlled by, the results of scientific inquiry. Cognate terms are *materialism* and *physicalism*. The former has traditionally meant 'all is matter'; the latter technically means reducible to the laws, particles, and forms of energy that physicists study.

Theism is the belief in the existence of God, an ultimate reality that transcends the universe as a whole. Passing over a few exceptions, Jews, Christians, Muslims, and Hindus are theists. When the term is used broadly, it includes pantheists, panentheists ('the world is in God'), and polytheists – hence most of the native African religions and the world's indigenous or tribal religions. Typically God is described as a personal being, often with the qualities of omniscience (all-knowing), omnipotence (all-powerful), and omnibenevolence (all-good). Based on the sacred scriptures of their particular tradition (the Bible, the Qur'an, the Upanishads), theists often ascribe other qualities to God, such as consciousness, love, justice, and righteousness.

Theists usually defend specific ways of knowing, distinct from science, through which humans are able to know something of God and God's nature. Traditionally, they have believed that God created the world, providentially guides it, and reveals God's self in it. This means that God does things in the world ('divine action'), carrying out actions that are either consistent with natural law or that involve setting natural regularities aside (miracles).

At first blush, theism and naturalism appear to be incompatible positions. Naturalists affirm that all that exists is the universe (or multiverse) and the objects within it, whereas theists claim that something transcends the universe. Naturalists generally use science as their primary standard for what humans know, whereas theists defend other ways of knowing as well, such as intuition or religious experience.

So let us explore. Are the two positions incompatible? Or, when one probes deeper, can one detect any deeper compatibilities? The best way to find out is to arrange a debate between a knowledgeable representative from each side and then to see what emerges. As you know, good debates between naturalists and theists in real life are hard to find; they often deteriorate into name-calling and shouting matches. Fortunately, in a book it is possible to imagine a calm and civil discussion between defenders of the two positions:

A NATURALIST AND A THEIST IN DEBATE

Host: The definitions of your positions have already been presented. So let me ask each of you to give a basic defense of your position. Let us start with the theist.

Theist: Religion is one of the oldest and most notable features of humanity. Some of the greatest wisdom and some of the most ennobling ethical ideals are contained in the world's religious traditions. These ideals are intrinsically linked to metaphysical beliefs, beliefs about the nature of ultimate reality. In my particular case, for example, I believe that an infinite personal being exists, one who is the Creator and ultimate ground of all finite things.

Naturalist: I don't dispute the role that religions played in the childhood and youth of our species. Indeed, although much evil has been done in the name of religion, I concede that it has sometimes also brought some good. But humanity in its maturity has invented science and begun to guide its decision-making by scientific results. If religion is to play any positive role today – and at least some of my naturalist friends believe it still can – it must function in whatever spaces are left over by the results of the various sciences.

T: There is no reason to think that the advent of science spells the death of religion. I advocate a more complex worldview, in which *both* serve important functions. I agree that religion should not compete with science in science's own proper domain, but many of the most important human questions lie outside the sphere of scientific competence.

Host: Thanks for those opening statements. Here's our next question. Are there areas of human experience, outside the domain of science, where religion provides knowledge?

T: Science describes what is but cannot tell us how we ought to act. Hence, ethics and morality lie outside its sphere. Science can tell us about the laws of nature and can explain the motion of physical bodies in the universe, but it cannot tell us what came before the universe or why it was created. Yet for many of us the meaning of human life turns on questions like these, questions about the ultimate nature of reality. Religion provides knowledge in these spheres.

N: You wrongly set limits on science, for example, by claiming that it has no moral implications. For example, there are values that arise in the process of doing science, and these provide good models for human interactions, for institutions, and for politics.[1] To know what kind of animal we have evolved to be tells us something about how we should live if we are to be happy and successful.

Hence science does provide some guidance for how humans ought to live. Of course, many human decisions are not dictated by physics or biology. In cases where there is great variability across cultures and moral systems, and where the beliefs in question do no damage, we can be relativists, allowing each person to choose for himself or herself. Religion falls in this category. And on the meaning question: I find meaning in the pursuit of knowledge about the world, as well as in my family, friends, and hobbies. What more meaning do I need?

Host: Okay, next question. Does anything exist beyond the natural world taken as a whole?

N: I think such questions are meaningless. We can observe empirical objects; we can measure them and make predictions about their causal interactions with each other. Why would we want to make truth claims about the existence of anything else? I tend to think that all such metaphysical language is literally meaningless – sort of like the famous poem from Lewis Carroll's *Alice in Wonderland*: ''Twas brillig and the slithy toves did gyre and gimble in the wabe...'

T: I think I can show that it's impossible to argue against metaphysics (in this case, belief in God) without *doing* metaphysics, and therefore contradicting oneself. I also think that a number of positive arguments can be given for affirming the existence of God. I don't actually share the view of a school called 'Intelligent Design,' which claims that these arguments are scientific arguments and can win in a head-to-head competition with contemporary scientific accounts of the world. They are to me instead *philosophical* arguments. But I think they are compelling nonetheless. I affirm the classical proofs for the existence of God: the ontological, cosmological, and teleological arguments. They do not *force* belief in the existence of God, but they at least show that it's not unreasonable to believe in God.

N: Those classic arguments are no longer persuasive in the scientific age. Some of them make assumptions about nature that we no longer hold today. For example, the teleological argument, the so-called argument from design, is no longer valid after Darwin. It argues that God exists based on the fact that animals and plants are matched to their environments; otherwise, it says, it would be impossible to explain why organisms are so perfectly suited to their surroundings. But Darwinism as a whole explains evolution and adaptation in scientific terms.

T: I agree that modern biology has rendered certain forms of the argument from design unconvincing. So let me give two arguments drawn from the context of modern science, which I think are still persuasive. The first is the 'fine-tuning' argument. We now know that the fundamental physical variables had to fall within a very narrow range for life to be possible, and in fact they do. This suggests that we live in an 'anthropic' universe – a universe designed for life, or at least the only kind of universe in which life could arise. As the cosmologist Edward Harrison writes somewhere, 'Here is the cosmological proof of the existence of God. The fine tuning of the universe provides prima facie evidence of deistic design. Take your choice: blind chance that requires multitudes of universes, or design that requires only one.'

My second argument moves from the existence of natural law to the existence of God. Natural laws are prior to the existence of physical states of affairs; they are the mathematical regularities that determine the motions of particles and specify the four fundamental forces in the universe. But if laws precede the existence of the universe, and laws are more mind-like than body-like, then *something like mind* is the more fundamental order of reality. This supports the idea that ultimate reality is God, not matter.

And some of the traditional arguments for the existence of God still remain valid in this age of science. One can only answer the question, 'Why is there something rather than nothing?' if there exists an ultimate reality that contains the reason for its existence within itself. God is such a being; therefore God exists (the cosmological proof). The existence of values and of our awareness of moral obligation proves that there must be a highest good, which is God or is grounded in God (the axiological proof). Finally, religious experience provides some evidence of the existence of God (the argument from mysticism or religious experience).

N: I know that nothing would please you more than to draw me into the morasses of your metaphysical debates. In truth, I find that whole way of speaking a throw-back to a bygone era. You know the standard criticisms of these arguments as well as I do. We could debate the issues until we're blue in the face, but there just isn't enough empirical evidence to decide the issue one way or the other. These are the kind of old-style metaphysical disputes that my friends and I are trying to break away from.

Let's take your last comment about religious experience. In a scientific age, shouldn't we try to learn as much as we can from the empirical study of religion? I don't need to argue that all of your sentences are literally meaningless, like the logical positivists once did, but I do want to encourage you and your co-religionists to learn everything that you can about religion by scientific means. Did religious beliefs and practices help human beings in their various clans and tribes to survive in hostile environments? If so, how did this happen? Did religion increase group cohesion and motivate people to obey the social mores necessary for their survival? If so, you and I can agree that religion helped people to adapt, at least in the earlier stages of human evolution.

Then we can discuss whether it is still adaptive today. If religion no longer is, why do people continue to believe? Perhaps religious belief is a by-product of mental and cognitive human traits that *are* adaptive – perhaps it's something that our brains produce when they are running in neutral, as it were. The brain's large prefrontal cortex functions to support generalizations and abstract reasoning. Maybe when it has no sense data to work with, it naturally produces the idea of God. Finally, can we agree that there are contexts in which religion is *maladaptive*, cases where religious practices decrease the fitness of a group? That question, too, could be studied empirically.

Such questions are only the start. Scientists are now studying how human biology shapes human feelings and desires (evolutionary psychology). There are biological explanations for why human beings believe certain things and disbelieve others. By studying evolutionary history, we can reconstruct the 'cognitive modules' around which human cognition is built. The cognitive study of religion today is beginning to identify the 'commonsense physics' and 'commonsense biology' that evolution has produced, as well as why it's intuitive for humans to detect agency in the world ... and in the heavens.

If we did turn to metaphysics, however, I would side with Richard Dawkins in *The God Delusion*. Evolution shows more complex organisms arising out of simpler states of affairs. This pattern suggests that the origin of all things was maximally simple. Theism, by contrast, begins with a maximally complex being, God, who then creates relatively simple processes. To my mind that puts theists at a disadvantage when it comes to the evidence.

T: I am interested in the empirical evidence as much as you are, but we interpret it very differently. If God exists, as I believe, is it surprising that our brains would be naturally wired to produce the idea of God? Wouldn't we also expect that groups that are bonded together by their belief in God would do better on this planet than non-religious groups? Also, you should know that traditional theism affirmed the doctrine of divine simplicity. So we are not at all disturbed by Richard Dawkins' argument; it merely asks us for what we already affirm.

Host: Thanks for that exchange; that was very helpful. What do the two of you believe about the nature of humanity?

T: Everything that exists is God's creation. We share many qualities with the animals as a result. Still, humans uniquely reflect the 'image of God.' Some people read Genesis in a literal way; they believe that God created humans as a 'special creation,' separate from God's creation of the animals. But others, like me, do not read the Hebrew Bible as a literal guide to scientific matters. We are happy to say that there was just the one creation of 'the heavens and the earth' and that humans evolved from animals. Still, I affirm that some unique human qualities have evolved through and out of this process. They include the ability to consciously know God and God's self-revelation, to know that we are morally responsible before others, to recognize our need for salvation and relationship with God, and to commit our lives to God's service. There is evidence that science is now helping to establish how unique many of the human capacities are.

N: Obviously I don't share your views on God, but in general, I would say, naturalists are more skeptical about claims for human uniqueness than you are. Evolution involves a process of many small (and some larger) mutations to a genome, which lead to differential survival rates of the offspring. It's true that new abilities evolve over time: the ability to move, sexual reproduction, the emergence of a brain and central nervous system, the ability to form mental representations of one's environment, culture and social bonding, and eventually the use of symbolic language. But it is a mistake to use any of these emergent properties as grounds for drawing an ontological divide and separating organisms into fundamentally different kinds of living beings.

Host: Next question. Is religion necessary for making life meaningful? Can religion alone produce the sense that we are 'at home in the universe'?

T: Here I think I am on especially strong ground. Science leads to nihilism, the sense that the world is ultimately meaningless or even absurd. On the assumption of naturalism, there is no purpose to our lives, no final direction to cosmic history. Science also cannot serve as the ground for values. One might *choose* to be moral, but one is not really obligated to do so. By contrast, if the world is created by a personal God who is good and who cares for creation, it's a very different picture. One gives alternate answers to the core questions of existence. Now there is meaning, purpose, directionality, and a real basis for distinguishing right from wrong.

N: Interestingly, I think I am on equally strong ground in answering our host's question. If physics were the only science, one might well conclude that all that exists is 'matter (and energy) in motion' as Thomas Hobbes wrote in the seventeenth century. But biology studies organisms, and every organism has at least one purpose in the world: to survive and reproduce. Some things are naturally more valuable to a given organism given its biology and (in some cases) culture.

T: But that's hardly a robust defense of values! If the fundamental value of nature is 'the survival of the fittest,' as Darwin wrote, then – to also quote Thomas Hobbes – the final state of man would be 'nasty, brutish, and short.' You might be able to show that treating your genetic relatives is biologically good, as is doing nice things for friends in the hope that they will reciprocate, but you could never ground a universal altruism – the call to love one's enemies, for example – on the basis of biology alone.

N: That's right; the call to universal love can be a cultural value, but it can't be derived from biology alone. But on the more general point, you and I disagree. Biology gives rise to culture, with its complex languages and symbol systems. The stories and the values we live by are among these cultural products. As a naturalist, I don't have to reduce everything in the natural world to genes or to the struggle for survival alone. I love my family and friends, pursue projects for the good of society, and hope for world peace just as much as you do; my values are as deeply embedded in who I am as yours are in you. It's just that I don't think they need any grounding outside of the natural and cultural worlds.

Host: Do miracles exist? Are the laws of nature ever suspended?

N: That one's easy: no! As the Scottish philosopher David Hume showed in his famous *Dialogues concerning Natural Religion* in the eighteenth century, the reasons against believing that a miracle has occurred, that natural laws have been suspended, will always be massively greater than the reasons for affirming one. Not only that; even the *possibility* of miracles occurring would make science as we know it impossible. Imagine that a scientist would have to say when she encountered an anomaly: 'Well, either my data is bad, or my theories are incomplete – or perhaps God has simply set aside a few natural laws here in order to actualize some goals in the world.' No science could be done in such a context. But since there is no scientific evidence that miracles have ever occurred, I rest easy on this one.

T: I think things are more complex than my friend describes. God could easily be influencing the world in myriad forms without being detected by microscopes or Geiger counters. Over the eons God could have guided the course of evolution in many ways. Even for those who don't believe that God directly brings about physical changes in the world, it is possible for God to subtly influence human thought (and perhaps animals too), allowing them to carry out God's will. For me the most important point is that God is *able* to work miracles in the world if and when God wishes. This possibility follows directly from God having created the finite world in the first place. The naturalist and I also disagree on the empirical question of whether miraculous things have happened. Haven't most of us heard stories and testimonies about some pretty miraculous events happening? Isn't it possible that they have? In the end, then, the most important thing for me is God's *ability* to act in the world.

Host: Our time is running out, and we must draw to a close. For the last question, let me ask you if you think that science and religion represent two opposing worldviews, or could they offer two complementary ways of construing the one reality?

T: Some of my Jewish, Christian, and Muslim friends think that their theism is incompatible with science; but I disagree, as you've heard. It's also true that many scientists tend to confuse the scientific data and theories themselves with their own anti-religious prejudices and secular worldview. When this occurs, they confuse science with atheism. When religious people hear scholars identifying science with atheism, is it surprising that they conclude that they have to be anti-scientific?

Still, I personally am not convinced that science and religion exclude each other. Accurate scientific knowledge of the natural world does not exclude the existence of a supernatural God. In my view, supernatural explanations *supplement* naturalistic ones. There is no ultimate inconsistency. How could there be, if God is the Creator of the heavens and the earth?

N: I too have many friends more radical than myself who affirm a complete incompatibility between science and all forms of religious belief. The media seems to love reporting on their views, and pays less attention to more moderate naturalists such as myself. I wouldn't want to say that science excludes *all religious belief whatsoever*. But I do think that my theist friend here, with his robust supernaturalist claims, is going to have a harder time reconciling his theology with science than, say, a Buddhist would have.

Nevertheless, the theist shouldn't derive too much comfort from my willingness to admit a compatibility-in-principle between science and religion. When it comes to concrete knowledge claims about God, I think there simply isn't enough empirical evidence to warrant your doctrines. If you want to affirm 'ultimate mystery' or stress the importance of living a 'spiritual' life, I can hardly complain. But as soon as you begin making any more concrete claims about God, I think you step beyond the empirical evidence.

T: I appreciate your open-mindedness. But your criterion, empirical evidence, begs the question against my position. If a God exists who is pure Spirit, then God will never be detected by the empirical means that you employ. God can only be known through metaphysical arguments, through the history of revelation (or scripture), through the sense of moral obligation, or through religious experience. If you rule out all four of those means in advance, of course it becomes impossible for me to defend my beliefs. If you include the appropriate paths to knowledge, then I maintain that there is ample evidence that God exists. When one looks across the world's religions and considers how deeply rooted religion is in human life, one realizes that there are some rather significant grounds for religious belief.

N: Actually, I think that the different religious traditions offer *very different* views of ultimate reality.

Host: That sounds like a great topic for us to come back to in later chapters of this book. For now, thanks for agreeing to appear in this book and to defend your views in such a clear and civil manner.

TAKING STOCK

What can we learn from this debate? First, it breaks at least one widespread stereotype: the tendency to associate all naturalists with science and all theists with an anti-scientific attitude. This is the first assumption many make in any discussion of science and religion; it is also one that is widely popularized in the media and in large-market books. Many people tend to identify science with an ultimate or 'metaphysical' naturalism; they then associate belief in God with an anti-scientific attitude.

Yet our short debate has already shown that such easy identifications are too simplistic. Our theist, at any rate, was interested in the results of science. He accepted evolution and incorporated it as part of his understanding of life on earth and of human beings. He grounded his arguments for the existence of God in data about the origin of the universe and its laws (cosmology). His understanding of God and the created world drew significantly from scientific results. Clearly, he saw science and religion as compatible, though not identical.

Nor did the naturalist fit the stereotype of a scientific naturalist, just as many scientists don't fit the stereotype either. She was not inherently antagonistic to religion or to broader metaphysical positions. Of course, she did greatly value empirical data and would not endorse any position that made the doing of science impossible. She also tended to be skeptical about metaphysical claims and did not herself believe in the existence of God or a higher power. But she manifested a sort of healthy agnosticism about such questions, rather than a virulent hostility toward them. She might even have said, 'Whatever religious or spiritual beliefs I end up affirming, I am concerned that they should not be in conflict with empirical results, for I want to learn as much as possible from scientific inquiry.'

Even this brief debate provides some sense of the range of possible positions. As we will soon see, the range only increases as we consider the vast differences between the world's major religious traditions. Some theists are deeply antagonistic toward all science, and some scientists are hostile toward all religion. We will look at the reasons that these two groups give for their views in the next chapter. But sometimes the roles are reversed. Many theists build the core ideas of their theism out of science. If this is true for theists, it holds all the more for non-theistic traditions such as Buddhism, as we will see in Chapter 3. Likewise, devotion to the practice of science need not make one anti-religious. Many scientists have pursued the practice of science out of deeply religious ends.

It will be our goal in the following chapters to explore the intricacy of the questions and the main answers that are being given to them today – to take this opening debate deeper, as it were. Instead of black and white connections, we will find a world of complex interconnections, of similarities and differences, of shared partnerships and sometimes conflicting projects. Readers will be encouraged to take their own positions on the various debates and to construct the best arguments they are able to construct. Sometimes you will resonate strongly with one or more of the existing positions in a given debate. At other times you may find yourself formulating and defending positions that no one has ever advanced before. Like all philosophical topics, this one admits of many different possible responses, which – ideally – will lead to ever deeper and more adequate answers.

But first, before the wider plains of discourse open up, we must cross the high mountains of the contemporary warfare between science and religion. One battle so powerfully exemplifies the two-sided case for the final incompatibility between science and religion, and continues to receive so much media attention, that it deserves a chapter of its own. I refer, of course, to the dramatic duel between 'intelligent design' theorists and the 'new atheists.'

QUESTIONS FOR REFLECTION AND DISCUSSION

1. Who do you think won this debate? Why?
2. If there was not a black and white winner, what do you think was the best argument that the theist brought? The best argument by the naturalist?
3. Were there any points in the debate where their beliefs were simply incommensurable – points at which they really could find no common ground on which to argue? See if you can identify two or three of these points.
4. Clearly, this naturalist and this theist were working with some conflicting assumptions. Can you identify some of these deeper-level assumptions? If the discussion partners brought them to the surface, do you think they could give reasons to support their own assumptions as more adequate than their opponent's assumptions?

Can you state their assumptions and then come up with some reasons of your own for or against their assumptions?

5. This was a remarkably civil debate: there was no name-calling, and both speakers stayed beautifully on topic. Are debates between naturalists and theists usually like this? If not, why not? What are some of the factors that helped to keep the conversation productive? To what extent are these factors present in 'real-life' debates between science and religion? How could the real-life debates be improved?

THE TWO MOST FAMOUS FOES

INTELLIGENT DESIGN *VERSUS* THE NEW ATHEISTS

The battles between religion and modern science go back to the dawn of the modern age. The famous empiricist Francis Bacon (1561–1626) already began to challenge traditional forms of religion, associating them with the 'idols of the theater':

> Lastly, there are idols which have immigrated into men's minds from the various dogmas of philosophies, and also from wrong laws of demonstration. These I call Idols of the Theatre; because in my judgment all the received systems are but so many stage-plays, representing worlds of their own creation after an unreal and scenic fashion. Nor is it only of the systems now in vogue, or only of the ancient sects and philosophies, that I speak: for many more plays of the same kind may yet be composed and in like artificial manner set forth; seeing that errors the most widely different have nevertheless causes for the most part alike.... And there is yet a third class [among the Idols of the Theatre], consisting of those who out of faith and veneration mix their philosophy and theology and traditions; among whom the vanity of some has gone so far aside as to seek the origin of science among spirits and genii.[1]

In the nineteenth century John Draper famously described the continuing warfare between science and religion:

> [T]he history of Science is not a mere record of isolated discoveries; it is a narrative of the conflict of two contending powers, the expansive force of the human intellect on one side, and the

compression arising from traditionary faith and human interests on the other.[2]

As a result, Andrew Dickson White called for a separation of the two powers:

> In all modern history, interference with science in the supposed interest of religion, no matter how conscientious such interference may have been, has resulted in the direst evils both to religion and science, and invariably; and, on the other hand, all untrammeled scientific investigation, no matter how dangerous to religion some of its stages may have seemed for the time to be, has invariably resulted in the highest good both of religion and science.[3]

While Draper and White were not opposed to religion as such, they believed that institutional religion should not interfere with science. There may be no black and white arguments that will resolve this centuries-long debate to the satisfaction of all concerned. Still, like the length of women's skirts, there definitely have been swings of fashion – times when the compatibility of science and religion has been emphasized, and other times when it has come under severe attack. The 1960s and 1970s saw the launch of an identifiable group of scholars studying the relationship between religion and science. Interestingly, the 1960s was also a period when Eastern approaches to unifying science and religion first began to gain a hearing in the West. The late 1990s was another such period, with many scientists beginning to make public statements and to publish books about the complementarity between the two. For a few years in the late 1990s, 100 new courses on religion and science were being launched each year.

In the years since the attacks on the World Trade Center on September 11, 2001, however, the trend has shifted in the opposite direction. Whether it was the frightening display of religious terrorism that tipped the scales, or whether the anti-evolution movements of 'Young Earth Creationism' and 'Intelligent Design' changed scientists' attitudes, is hotly disputed. In any event, the last years have seen the birth of a major international movement known as the 'New Atheism.' The more attention the New

Atheists garner, the more religious people seem to be attracted to Intelligent Design.

Both Intelligent Design and the New Atheism have their more moderate and their more radical adherents. It is the task of this chapter to explore the arguments (or, where arguments are missing, the rhetoric) of the two warring camps. This debate is being played out in the media, on blog sites, and in the public domain as a war to the death. At the end, each side hopes, only one contestant will remain standing. As you read, try to determine which group has the most convincing arguments. Where would you locate yourself, and why? Or, if your view is missing in this chapter, can you set up the discussion in a different way altogether, so that a place is created for the sort of position you want to defend?

Not all of the chapters will be as oppositional as this one. Still, before we move further into our study, it is important first to evaluate the case for a complete opposition between science and religion. Many religious persons, and many scientists, for example, resist this way of setting up the debate. The only way to evaluate their defenses of the compatibility of science and religion is to first formulate the antagonism in its strongest form. Some will find themselves clearly on one particular side or the other in the following few pages. Others will leave this chapter with the desire to find precisely the sorts of mediating positions that both sides here are seeking to eliminate.

INTELLIGENT DESIGN

Intelligent Design is an extremely influential movement found especially in the more conservative wings of all three of the Abrahamic religions. At first glance, the movement appears simply to stand for the very basic claim (a claim shared by Jews, Christians, and Muslims) that there is a Creator God whose creative intent lies behind the universe. Yet in Intelligent Design theory, or 'ID,' this core religious belief is combined with the sense that recent science has become a major opponent to belief in God. In particular, the leaders of the movement argue that the standard Darwinian picture of the evolution of life is incompatible with, and indeed actively hostile toward, any belief in God. As Phillip Johnson, one of the founders of the ID movement, has written:

As the Darwinists move out to convert the nation's school children to a naturalistic outlook, it may become more and more difficult to conceal the religious implications of their system. Plenty of people within the Darwinist camp know what is being concealed, and cannot be relied upon to maintain a discreet silence.[4]

The role of ID is to offer an alternative account of the natural world to the standard Darwinian account. Unlike some religious thinkers, however, their response to the 'threat' of Darwin is not to eschew all science and to argue for a different position that is grounded in faith. Instead, ID offers a view of the origin of the universe and of the evolution of life that its proponents claim *should actually be understood as science* – alongside, yet in competition with, the standard scientific accounts. In the past this alternative science was known as 'Creation Science' or 'Young Earth Creationism.' There is some evidence that scholars at the Discovery Institute, one of the main supporters of Creation Science, intend Intelligent Design to communicate some of the same conclusions as Creation Science. But now they want to give scientifically compelling grounds for these conclusions, rather than basing them on religious arguments alone.[5]

ID as science

Intelligent Design, in other words, is meant to function as a scientific hypothesis. For example, it omits any language about God or the Creator. Its defenders argue that, since it is a science, it should be included in scientific textbooks and taught as an alternative theory in classes on astronomy, cosmology, and especially biology. This, at any rate, is the argument that was used by the lawyers for the defense in a highly publicized trial in Dover, Pennsylvania; it was also used in defending Intelligent Design before the Kansas School Board and the Texas School Board. As Phillip Johnson once wrote on the Access Research Network website, '[Intelligent Design] means we affirm that God is objectively real as creator, that the reality of God is tangibly recorded in evidence accessible to science, particularly in biology.'

This attitude of being anti-science and yet offering an alternative scientific position is part of what makes Intelligent Design difficult to place. Perhaps the best way to proceed is to identify the core underlying intuition of ID, then its connection with contemporary science, and then the concrete arguments that are used by ID theorists. The first task is easy. The basic intuition is that the universe evidences design. Clearly, things that evidence design must have a designer. So behind the appearances must lie an intelligent designer. The role of ID science, then, is to study those parts of the universe that give the greatest evidence of having been designed.

In Chapter 1 we observed how the theist appealed to fine-tuning: the fact that, if the fundamental constants of the universe were different by even an extremely tiny amount, life could never have arisen. The cosmologist Bernard Carr draws a similar conclusion:

> One would have to conclude that either the features of the universe invoked in support of the Anthropic Principle are only coincidence or that the universe was indeed tailor-made for life. I will leave it to the theologians to ascertain the identity of the tailor.

From here ID theorists move on to more specific arguments. Let us consider two of the most famous examples. The first one is the 'information theory' argument advanced by William Dembski. He writes:

> Intelligent design can be unpacked as a theory of information. Within such a theory, information becomes a reliable indicator of design as well as a proper object for scientific investigation.... My broad conclusion is that information is not reducible to natural causes, and that the origin of information is best sought in intelligent causes. Intelligent design, thereby, becomes a theory for detecting and measuring information, explaining its origin, and tracing its flow.[6]

Dembski uses arguments drawn from mathematics, and in particular from probability theory. He tries to show quantitatively that the amount of information in the universe could not have been produced by unguided evolution, say, by fluctuations in the initial quantum vacuum or by the Darwinian mechanisms of random variation and selective retention within the biosphere. Hence it is empirically (scientifically) more adequate to postulate a conscious agent who intentionally created the natural order.

The second major approach has been advanced by Michael Behe. Behe argues:

> Darwin's theory of evolution prospered by explaining much of the data of his time and the first half of the 20th century, but my article will show that Darwinism has been unable to account for phenomena uncovered by the efforts of modern biochemistry during the second half of this century. I will do this by emphasizing the fact that life at its most fundamental level is irreducibly complex and that such complexity is incompatible with undirected evolution.[7]

In *Darwin's Black Box*, Behe provided a number of details to bolster his scientific case:

> [A]s biochemists have begun to examine apparently simple structures like cilia and flagella, they have discovered staggering complexity, with dozens or even hundreds of precisely tailored parts. It is very likely that many of the parts we have not considered here are required for any cilium to function in a cell. As the number of required parts increases, the difficulty of gradually putting the system together skyrockets, and the likelihood of indirect scenarios plummets. Darwin looks more and more forlorn.[8]

Biochemistry, he says, offers many examples of 'irreducible complexity'; that is, of complex natural systems that *could not* have been constructed gradually over many generations. Darwinian explanations work only if each stage in the evolution of a complex phenomenon (say, red blood cells) adds to the 'fitness' of the organism in its environment. But red blood cells would not have helped the organism's fitness, Behe says, until they reached their fully developed form and could actually carry oxygen. Hence there is *and could be* no Darwinian explanation for their evolution. Only an Intelligent Designer could have created such structures. So the better science is one that includes the hypothesis of intelligent design.

But is it really science?

It is fair to say that ID has not fared well in the scientific literature. ID theorists themselves admit that their work has not been published in refereed scientific journals. But, they respond, the fault lies with the scientific community, which is unfairly conspiring to exclude them. Scientists' prejudices for materialism and against the Intelligent Designer hypothesis have kept them from giving the ID arguments a fair hearing. Therefore, nothing about the truth or falsity of ID can be inferred from its rejection within the scientific community.

One should never underestimate the human ability at self-deception, and pre-existing beliefs *do* often prejudice our hearing of new data. Still, even with the most charitable attitude, it is rather hard to ascribe ID's difficulties to prejudice alone. Serious criticisms have been raised about each of the major ID examples. Yet powerful answers simply haven't been forthcoming. ID does not seem to have become an empirically productive research program.

Of course, it is always hard to launch a completely new research program in science, since existing areas of research tend to garner higher levels of financial support. But, again, struggling scientists have always managed to get the word out about experimental breakthroughs that challenge existing paradigms; word has spread; and eventually the institution of science catches on. In the case of ID, there doesn't seem to have been significant new empirical data. Paul Nelson wrote in 2004, 'Easily the biggest challenge facing the ID community is to develop a full-fledged theory of biological design. We don't have such a theory right now, and that's a problem.' A year later Michael Behe said, 'there are no peer reviewed articles by anyone advocating for intelligent design supported by pertinent experiments or calculations which provide detailed rigorous accounts of how intelligent design of any biological system occurred.'

These failures notwithstanding, ID continues to spread and to win advocates. Over 50 percent of American evangelicals say that they do not believe in (Darwinian) evolution. Intelligent Design has massive support in the Muslim world; estimates are that it represents the majority view there as well. If scientific success does not explain its popularity, something else must account for the amazing growth and resilience of this movement. Technical work by Intelligent Design theorists includes some very specific scientific arguments, but the arguments by themselves don't suffice to account for its growing popularity.

One can only conclude that the core intuition of ID represents a deep conviction for many people who believe in God. Specifically, the vast majority of Jews, Christians, Muslims, and Hindus believe that God, the ultimate origin and ground of reality, is intelligent, conscious, and Creator of the universe. 'Designer,' then, is for them an appealing way to affirm that God is, in some sense or another, responsible for the universe as a whole – and thus for the beauty, order, and regularity that we discover within it.

Could it be, then, that the real insight of ID is this intuition of design, and that the claim that ID is an empirical science represents a mistake? As soon as one recognizes that ID actually consists of two distinct claims, it becomes possible to examine them separately. It turns out, upon reflection, that the sense (which many humans share) that there is some sort of design or order in the universe can be affirmed in very different ways.

Consider these four. First, someone might have a private or subjective response to the universe, say, as she walks under a starry sky at night-time. She might say,

> I can't help but feel that there must be some intelligence behind it. After all, how could such beauty and order have come about all by itself? I'm not even sure this is an argument at all, but it is certainly a part of my basic feeling about this universe in which I live.

In this case, someone reports a basic intuition about her experience and does not claim to show others' views to be false.

Second, this belief might function as part of the language of a given religious community, without members of that community trying to turn it into a universal argument that all persons are supposed to accept. Imagine that someone finds herself with a basic religious faith as part of her core response to the world. Imagine that she begins to reflect about her religious faith, trying to understand it and to formulate what it means to her. Already in the twelfth century Anselm of Canterbury called this approach 'faith seeking understanding' (*fides quaerens intellectum*). Certain core beliefs about the world, such as that it was created and designed by God, might be a part of the 'confessional' language of a religious tradition – the language used in hymns and creeds and confessions and sermons and worship services. Here again, one could use this language without making any claims to possess a universally valid philosophical argument.

Third, one might engage in what believers call 'apologetics' or 'the defense of the faith.' Apologetic arguments are philosophical arguments that are meant to be persuasive to philosophers and other persons who don't share the faith in question. Obviously, these arguments make stronger claims than the first two options above. For example, one might claim that they represent universally valid philosophical arguments. Still, one could make this assertion without claiming that his results are scientific.

But fourth and finally, one might also make an even stronger affirmation. Someone might claim that his arguments are not only *philosophically* valid, but that they are also *scientifically* valid. This last move amounts to the claim that the hypothesis that the universe is created or designed *makes for a better scientific explanation than does natural science (as we know it) as a whole*. Intelligent Design in this fourth sense – but only in this sense – would stand as a rival hypothesis to the standard scientific method and the standard scientific accounts of the universe. Only this fourth option claims to have better credentials for being accepted by all those who seek scientific explanations for the universe. As we have seen, supporters of Intelligent Design do explicitly make this fourth claim for the ID position and its supporting arguments.

The tragedy is that many people who mean to affirm the first, second, or third position are led to believe that the only way they can do this is by making the fourth, the scientific claim. There is something sad, even tragic, about this outcome. Theists may or may not succeed in the end at constructing philosophical arguments in defense of the intuition of design. But instead of concentrating on that task – which is arguably their more urgent task – they have been led into what turns out to be a fruitless quest for scientific legitimation for their claims. Surely this mistake (if it is indeed, as I think, a mistake) is one of the interesting lessons in the religion–science discussion of recent years.

GOD, DESIGN, AND DELUSION

The quickest way to get a sense for what are the New Atheist views on religion is to let Richard Dawkins speak for himself. (Unless otherwise noted, the quotations are from his recent *The God Delusion*.)

- 'God, in the sense defined, is a delusion; and, as later chapters will show, a pernicious delusion.'[9]
- 'I am not attacking any particular version of God or gods. I am attacking God, all gods, anything and everything supernatural, wherever and whenever they have been or will be invented' (36).
- When you reject religion, 'you stand to lose comforting delusions: you can no longer suck at the pacifier of faith in immortality' (*Devil's Chaplain*, 13).
- 'The deist God is certainly an improvement over the monster of the Bible. Unfortunately it is scarcely more likely that he exists, or ever did. In any of its forms the God Hypothesis is unnecessary' (46).
- 'Fundamentalist religion is hell-bent on ruining the scientific education of countless thousands of innocent, well-meaning, eager young minds. Non-fundamentalist, "sensible" religion may not be doing that. But it is making the world safe for fundamentalism by teaching children, from their earliest years, that unquestioning faith is a virtue' (286).
- In Christianity and Islam, 'you don't have to make the case for what you believe. If somebody announces that it is part of his faith, the rest of society, whether of the same faith, or another, or of none, is obliged, by ingrained custom, to "respect" it without question; respect it until the day it manifests itself in a horrible massacre like the destruction of the World Trade Center, or the London or Madrid bombings' (306).
- 'Faith is an evil precisely because it requires no justification and brooks no argument.... Faith can be very very dangerous, and deliberately to implant it into the vulnerable mind of an innocent child is a grievous wrong' (308).

Unfortunately, the ramped-up rhetoric has led to some equally sharp language in response. I cite just one example. The Christian philosopher, Alvin Plantinga, has written a sharp rejoinder entitled 'The Dawkins Confusion: Naturalism *ad absurdum*.'[10] There he writes,

> Richard Dawkins is not pleased with God: 'The God of the Old Testament is arguably the most unpleasant character in all of fiction. Jealous and proud of it; a petty, unjust, unforgiving control-freak; a vindictive, bloodthirsty ethnic-cleanser; a misogynistic, homophobic, racist, infanticidal, genocidal, fili-cidal, pestilential, megalomaniacal....' Well, no need to finish the quotation; you get the idea. Dawkins seems to have chosen God as his sworn enemy. (Let's hope for Dawkins' sake God doesn't return the compliment.)

SIX NEW ATHEIST ARGUMENTS

One may well find oneself stymied by the stalemate between the New Atheists and their opponents. When one of the best-known science writers of our day writes a book on evolution and religion, one would expect to find a pretty serious argument. Yet, if his opponents are to be believed, Dawkins fails to make any serious case at all.[11] Can that be right? In order to find out, I suggest that we take a moment to look at Dawkins' major publications over the last several decades, looking for the underlying arguments that, taken together, present his best case against religion. Here are the six most significant arguments I could reconstruct out of his books:

• *Argument #1: Religion is not supported by any evidence at all.* In *River Out of Eden* Dawkins argues that

> Science shares with religion the claim that it answers deep questions about origins, the nature of life, and the cosmos. But there the resemblance ends. Scientific beliefs are *supported by evidence*, and they get results. Myths and faiths are not and do not.[12]

It would indeed be a deep problem if religious beliefs are completely irrational as a matter of principle. But is it true that scientific conclusions are always based on good evidence, whereas people hold religious beliefs for no good reasons at all? Certainly one can find religious persons who seem to hold beliefs without any serious consideration of the reasons for and against them. '*Credo quia absurdum*,' as the old Latin phrase has it: 'I believe because it is absurd.' (In fact, no major theologian ever made this assertion, though St. Anselm in the twelfth century did affirm, '*Credo ut intelligam*,' which means 'I believe *in order to* understand.')

Most religious persons would say that they base their beliefs on different *kinds* of evidence than the natural sciences produce. If one wants to argue that *only one kind of evidence* is admissible as evidence – natural scientific evidence – then he has a rather difficult case on his hands. After all, in daily human existence we accept radically different kinds of evidence for different purposes. One standard of evidence holds for whether my daughter took a chocolate from the chocolate box, and quite another is required to convict a person of first-degree murder in a court of law. Both are distinct from your evidence that your partner loves you or that you had breakfast this morning. It is an interesting and subtle question to ask what kind of evidence *could* show, even in principle, that our world is religiously significant, or that we are 'at home' in the universe, or that our fundamental values correspond with reality.

- *Argument #2: Biology disproves religion*. Again in *River Out of Eden* Dawkins argues, 'if there is only one Creator who made the tiger and the lamb, the cheetah and the gazelle, what is He playing at? Is He a sadist who enjoys spectator blood sports?' (105). A few pages later he moves from rhetorical questions to his core assertion:

> The universe we observe has precisely the properties we should expect if there is, at bottom, no design, no purpose, no evil and no good, nothing but blind, pitiless indifference.

> (133)

Now it is probably not true that the universe has *none* of the properties that would be consistent with purpose. Many scientists have written about the 'fine-tuning' of the universe: the fact that many of the fundamental constants fall within that extremely narrow range of values which alone would allow life to emerge.[13] In addition, there are features in the emergence and organization of life and consciousness that suggest something more than 'blind, pitiless indifference.'

Yet the problem of evil *is* serious. Random, arbitrary suffering is indeed not what one would expect in a universe created by a good God. Nor, one supposes, is the extinction of 99 percent of all the species that ever lived. These are serious issues. Not surprisingly, theists have indeed taken them seriously. Powerful responses to the challenges of evil and suffering, called 'theodicies,' have been composed. It may be that every attempt that theists make to justify the amount of evil in the world fails, but a serious critic will have to *show* that they fail. From reading some of the New Atheists, one would never know that any theodicies have been written, much less that there is a serious, ongoing debate on the topic.

- *Argument #3: Beware of all questions that are not biological questions.* In *Unweaving the Rainbow* Dawkins writes:

> Gould's eternally unresolved questions in paleontology are three in number: Does time have a directional arrow? Is the driving motor of evolution internal or external? Does evolution proceed gradually or in sudden jumps?... All three of Gould's eternal metaphors are bad poetry, forced analogies that obscure rather than illuminate.[14]

What irritates Dawkins most about these three questions? Dawkins himself lets us know what bothers him the most about Gould's questions. Apparently, it is *that they cannot be resolved within the context of Darwinian thought.* As Gould – correctly! – notes, they '*preceded* evolutionary thought and found no resolution within the Darwinian paradigm' (ibid.).

Now look again at the questions. They are some of the deep, enduring questions about the human condition. These questions have been asked, in one way or another, wherever humans have developed culture, writing, and art. At first sight, Dawkins appears to be the one calling us back to humility. But critics see this differently. Where is there *less* humility, they ask, and where is there greater presumptuousness: in those who wonder about enduring questions such as these three; or in those, like Dawkins, who claim to *know* that these questions are meaningless, 'bad poetry'? If you have a friend who is tone-deaf and dislikes music, his disdain does not prove that Mozart and Beethoven are worthless composers. If science is going to replace the natural human drive to reflect on ever-broader questions and to wonder about ultimate issues, it will take some rather more serious work than the simple assertion that non-scientific questions are meaningless.

• *Argument #4.* As you read your way further into Dawkins' life work, you may find yourself increasingly curious: if he has made a mistake, what exactly is the mistake that he has made? What has convinced him that all non-scientific reflection is irrational? It is an intriguing question and one that, as far as I can tell, has occurred to few of his critics. Let me put it in more provocative form: if Dawkins were a great philosopher, and if he were to give his objection to religious knowledge claims its most power-ful formulation, what would that objection be?

The answer may lie in a book appropriately titled *A Devil's Chaplain: Reflections on Hope, Lies, Science, and Love.* In one passage Dawkins reflects on the 'exacting, well-honed rules' by which science proceeds. Many scholars share his sense that great science often *does* manifest these virtues in an impressive manner:

> testability, evidential support, precision, quantifiability, consistency, intersubjectivity, repeatability, universality, progressiveness, independence of cultural milieu, and so on.

(145)

But then look at what he tacks on to the end of this list: 'Faith spreads despite a *total lack* of *every single one of these* virtues.'

Perhaps there lies the answer. Could it be that Dawkins tends to see the world in a completely black-and-white fashion (in exactly the fashion, I suppose, that he thinks religious people see the world)? Science works by purely rational means; but religion stands for everything that is irrational, backward-looking, obscu-rantist – in short: evil. Is it surprising that religion comes out as evil in Dawkins' scheme, given that he defines it from the outset as the antithesis to everything good?

- *Argument #5.* In *The Devil's Chaplain*, in a perfect one-two punch, Dawkins combines his framework of good-versus-evil, science-versus-religion with what critics say is the 'straw man' fallacy. He does not consider any constructive partnerships between scientists and philosophers or theologians today. The only alternative he acknowledges is the view that science and religion converge into a complete identity. He then shows that this convergence or identity relationship is unlikely and would do damage to science. This (obviously silly) possibility he dismisses with a quick insult: 'Convergence? Only when it suits. To an honest judge, the alleged convergence between religion and science is a shallow, empty, hollow, spin-doctored sham' (*Devil's Chaplain*, 151). In short, the only choice is between science and ... the Dark Side. That leaves us with the conclusion that, for rational persons, it is science or nothing.

- *Argument #6.* This may help to explain Dawkins' claim that, if a 'why' question cannot be answered by science, it cannot be answered at all. You have the right, he tells us, 'to ask the "Why" question of a bicycle's mudguards or the Kariba Dam, but at the very least you have no right to *assume* that the "Why" question deserves an answer when posed about a boulder, a misfortune, Mt. Everest or the universe. Questions can be simply inappropriate, however heartfelt their framing' (*River Out of Eden*, 97).

What about this sixth and final argument? One response is that the existence of a human who is encouraged not to wonder in the face of the universe is a truncated existence. A person who is not allowed to ask why 'misfortune' strikes is a person who cannot grieve, and reflect on that grief, and then come to some sort of peace about the meaning of her existence in a world like ours. *Must* one conclude that all reflection outside of science is vacuous? One might believe, for example, that contemporary biology offers the best explanation of the evolution of the biosphere that humans have ever possessed. But does that mean that one should then cease to ask the broader philosophical and religious questions that humans ask about their existence: is there a purpose or goal? Am I more than my biological drives, such as my drives for sex and aggression? Can I only love my neighbor, or does it make sense to (try to) love my enemies as well? These *look* like vital questions about human existence. Must we exclude them as meaningless?

Of course, the *right to ask* – indeed the crucial importance of asking – these broader sorts of questions is not an excuse to put forward dogmatic answers or to claim certainty for one's guesses. I once debated with a professor who believed he *knew* why God allowed the Holocaust, in which some six million Jews (and millions of others) were brutally killed by the Nazis. He even knew *whom* God was punishing and *why* God was punishing them in this way, and he could tell you why God was completely just in allowing, or even causing, these actions. I found the theories of this professor not only implausible but, in a disturbing way, also immoral. That aside, one wonders: how could he be so certain? The right to ask life's biggest questions does not give you *carte blanche* to pass off just any guess as gospel. Some religious beliefs are really wrong – factually wrong, and, most would agree, ethically wrong as well. But must we therefore conclude that *every* philosophical musing, every spiritual response, every religious hypothesis that humans formulate when they stare at the stars or witness a baby's birth is misguided, demeaning … incompatible with good empirical science, and ultimately irrational?

HOW DAWKINS *SHOULD* HAVE ARGUED

We have reconstructed six of Richard Dawkins' arguments and explored some initial criticisms. When interpreting other authors, scholars are supposed to use something called 'the principle of charity of interpretation.' It is the idea that you look for the strongest possible interpretation of another's text. (Dawkins' critics ought to follow this principle, whether or not he follows it himself.) So what are the best ways that he *might* have argued?

Consider the following three possibilities. First, perhaps Dawkins thinks that the successes of biology render it *impossible* that a God should exist who is in any way involved with the fate of this cosmos after the moment of creation. That would amount to the claim that, if evolutionary biology is true, then theism is false. The most one could have, on this view, would be *deism*. Deism is the view that some intelligence may have created the universe at the very beginning – 'with a snap of his fingers,' as Blaise Pascal once wrote – but that this intelligence has exercised no influence on the world whatsoever since that time. (This is the view, for example, that underlies Paul Davies' widely read book, *The Mind of God*.)

The second possibility is that religion, though possible, is evidentially inferior. Perhaps Dawkins thinks that the evidence provided by the biological sciences renders it improbable, or very improbable, or (this would come closer to the tone of his writings) *extremely* improbable that any God played a role in the origins of life or in its subsequent evolution. This would be an 'evidentialist' argument, that is, an argument about probabilities and improbabilities. Now we know that evidentialist arguments never produce certainties, since even what is highly improbable *might* still turn out to be true. If Dawkins intends this sort of argument – and there are many signs in his writings that he does – then perhaps he has just overstated his conclusions a little. Perhaps what he *means* to say is that, although God *might* play a role in evolution, he (Dawkins) thinks it highly unlikely that God does so.

Finally, perhaps Dawkins does not mean to base his case on any *results* of science at all, but rather *on the methods and mindset of science*. That is, perhaps he is trying to say that when one 'thinks like a scientist' he or she cannot at the same time hold any sort of religious faith. Religion is based on irrational trust, untestable private experience, or the blind acceptance of authority (or so Dawkins assumes), whereas science is based on objective evidence and critical inquiry. And never the twain shall meet. On this theory, it is not that anything in biology disproves God; it might well be that the actual results of the biological sciences – genetics and proteomics and population biology – are fully compatible with at least some forms of religious belief. (Religious belief being as diverse as it is, it's hard to imagine how this could *not* be the case!)

Instead, maybe Dawkins thinks that the problem lies in the *cognitive styles* associated with religious belief. Perhaps he believes that they are in tension with the cognitive styles of science, indeed so deeply and even essentially in tension that the two simply cannot cohabitate in the same person. Perhaps the mere existence of people with 'the religious cognitive style' (whatever that might be) is so insidious and so destructive to the development of good scientific minds that the mere *existence* of religion is a threat to the future of science.

These are interesting arguments, and it does seem that the New Atheists' case will have to depend on one or more of them. Now that we have them clearly before us, let us see how they stand up.

Biology excludes the idea of God

How does the first argument stand up? Well, it's a little difficult to see how the truth of anything like the contemporary science of evolution *necessarily* excludes the existence of God. Suppose you accept the validity of (something like) the current evolutionary synthesis. You would then place the burden of proof on those, such as the advocates of Intelligent Design, who wish to jettison the last 150 years of progress in biological science. But why would you then think that biology *necessarily* excludes God?

Necessity arguments have a peculiar feature: if you can find *even one* plausible alternative, then the necessity claim becomes unjustified. (Probability arguments, we will see in a moment, are a very different kettle of fish.) If I make the universal claim, 'All swans are white,' and you can show me even one black swan, then my claim was false. Necessity claims are even stronger than universal claims. 'Necessarily true' means 'cannot possibly be false.' When you assert, 'Chess is necessarily played with a set of black pieces against a set of white pieces,' you are claiming that there is no viable way in which a game could be chess without black and white pieces. Hence if it is even plausible that chess would still be chess when played with red and black pieces (as it obviously is!), then your claim is undercut.

So here is one plausible alternative to this first argument. Imagine that some Intelligence, some ground of being with the attribute of mind or consciousness, preceded the big bang (or whatever was the origin of the cosmos). Imagine that it exercises a sort of 'lure' toward increased complexity. Now this lure could well be *compatible* with the causal properties of matter and energy as we know them, yet without being *reducible* to that causality. (At least since Aristotle, philosophers have debated the existence and functions of this sort of 'final causality.' Many have argued that the existence of final causality is fully compatible with physical causes and with the pursuit of empirical science as long as certain conditions are met.[15]) No law of physics would be invalidated by a divine lure toward complexity. In fact, the laws of nature allow for an increase in complexity as much as they presuppose uniformity in nature and across the universe. Certainly the history of life offers unmistakable evidence that life forms do in fact grow increasingly complex, so the principle is not completely without evidence.

Note that this response does not actually show that such a divine lure toward increasing complexity exists. All that is required, the defender says, is that this idea of a divine lure be a *plausible* theory (which includes being compatible with the results of evolutionary biology as we know them). It looks like it is. And as long as there is at least one plausible theory that fulfills the conditions, the defender concludes, it is a mistake to claim that biology *necessarily* presupposes the non-existence of God. Is he right?

Biology renders the existence of God improbable

What about Dawkins' second argument, the probabilistic or 'evidentialist' argument? When one thinks about the possibility we have just considered, the possibility of a divine lure, one begins to recognize how difficult it is to make firm probability assessments about the existence of God. By what measure would one become certain that no God exists?

The first problem concerns the dataset: what data are relevant to this question, and how do they change over time? It turns out that the probabilities vacillate greatly depending on when in the history of biology one raises the question. I suppose one would have to say that the probability of God was higher prior to the discovery of the double-helix structure by Watson and Crick in 1953. At that time many might say it decreased, because biologists now knew more about the structures by which genetic information was transmitted naturally (that is, without divine assistance). Should one then say that it decreased even more when more scientists became convinced that the Nobel Prize-winner Jacques Monod was right and that 'pure chance, absolutely free but blind, is at the very root of the stupendous edifice of evolution'?[16] Or should we say that Monod's judgment was a philosophical prejudice and not an argument at all, and hence the probabilities remain unchanged? Should we say that the odds of God's existence decreased with the funding of the Human Genome Project, but then increased again with the discovery that the human genome contains significantly fewer than 30,000 genes?

One begins to sense the difficulty of attempting to make quantitative judgments about the probability of God based on the results of science at any given moment. Some allege that it is a kind of 'category mistake' to move directly from biological results to the conclusion that no intelligent cause could have pre-existed the big bang. They claim that one may also argue in the *opposite* direction from Dawkins. Clearly, discovering the chemical structure of the DNA molecule taught us more about how complexity increased in the history of this planet. Perhaps the increase in complexity is a macro-pattern that runs across evolution and there are other such patterns, such as a trend toward more intelligent organisms. Perhaps those patterns are discernible only at a higher scale – indeed, perhaps only at a scale that includes philosophical or theological concepts. Then again, perhaps not. *But how would we know*, from something as specific as the discovery of DNA, what is the correct level of study at which higher-scale patterns might be discerned? It is difficult to show that evolutionary biology provides the *sole and complete* explanation for all biological phenomena.

Dawkins' argument for the improbability of God turns on the belief that biology is complete. But, other critics respond, how could one ever show that biology is complete based on biology alone? In the end, they argue, it is misguided to use evolutionary biology to determine the probability of God, given the vacillations within biology itself. (Of course, this conclusion cuts two ways: against Dawkins on the one side, and against Intelligent Design advocates on the other, who would use biology to prove the existence of God.) How would one ever determine the likelihood of *any* particular metaphysical explanation based only on biological (or chemical or physical) results? Here is a case, they say, of comparing apples and oranges if ever there was one!

One important possibility remains. It would seem that the more complete biological explanations are – the more they can account for *everything* – the more unnecessary higher-order explanations become. That brings us to Dawkins' third and final argument.

Religious belief is incompatible with the scientific mindset

We know that Dawkins believes that religious belief is incompatible with the scientific mindset, but why should we think his belief is true? In the end, his incompatibility claim will hold *only if all adequate knowledge is scientific knowledge*. That is, it will hold only if what *seem* to be non-scientific forms of knowledge – say, in theology, philosophy, and the humanities in general – turn out in the end to be nothing more than vague manifestations of a much more rigorous form of knowledge, the kind of knowledge that natural scientists obtain.

Put differently, Dawkins' incompatibility claim presupposes the doctrine of *explanatory reductionism*. It presupposes that each level of explanation can be reduced downward, at least in principle, until ultimately all explanations are given at the most fundamental level: the level of genes (in biological systems) or microphysics (in physical systems). Should we accept this reductionistic assumption?

Before we move to explicitly religious questions, perhaps it would be wise first to (try to) locate some more neutral ground. So let us examine Dawkins' thesis of downward reduction using the test case of psychology. By psychology I mean those theories that, whatever else they contain, also make essential reference to the intentions of human actors. If psychology is reducible to biology, then there *is* no essential reference to actors' intentions. Instead, every explanation that refers to human intentions can be paraphrased, without loss of explanatory value, by explanations given in terms of brain chemistry, neuronal firings, or the history of evolutionary biology. Are there any good reasons to conclude that the reduction of psychological explanations to biology cannot be carried out, even in principle?

Two such reasons have been put forward in the literature: the dynamics of culture, and the role of mental representations and intentions. Let us look at culture first. As soon as cultural patterns begin to emerge and influence behavior, it appears that strictly biological accounts need to be supplemented by another type of explanation. Where cultures influence behavior, knowledge is transmitted from one generation to another by teaching and learning and not only by genetic inheritance. Culture is thus 'Lamarckian,' which means that it allows parents to pass on traits to their offspring that they acquired during their lifetime. By contrast, the biological sciences today are Darwinian (or, more technically, neo-Darwinian) *rather than* Lamarckian. Genes transmit biological information from parents to child, and the basic genetic structure is not changed by events that occur during the lifetime of the parent. (In fact, Richard Dawkins' early book, *The Selfish Gene*, is one of the works that encouraged biologists to insist on this criterion as the defining feature of biological orthodoxy.)

If that is right, cultural learning, and the cultural beliefs it produces, are not fully captured by the dynamics of genes. Yet culture deeply influences both current behavior and subsequent biological history. Take a simple example: at one time most of the human race could not absorb lactose, the sugar found in milk, other than from a human mother. Today a much higher percentage of people can absorb lactose from various dairy sources, although this ability still varies dramatically across populations. The evolution of the enzymes for absorbing lactose is of course a biological process. And yet a variety of *cultural* factors also influenced this biological effect, including the practice of herding animals, access to fresh milk, the development of dairying technology, and whether drinking fresh milk is valued and encouraged. A variety of cultural and religious attitudes affected the biological evolution of lactose tolerance; evolving lactose tolerance in turn encouraged the further development of these forms of culture.[17] This reciprocal influence of two very different forms of evolution is known as the *co-evolution* of biology and culture.

It turns out that culture, in this sense, is vastly more widespread in the animal kingdom than we ever imagined. Many animals learn behaviors from their parents that are not genetically programmed. In fact, there are good biological reasons for animals to rely so extensively on other kinds of learning to supplement genetically programmed behavior. Consider the comments of Ernst Mayr and Jürgen Nicolai:

> 'The great selective advantage of a capacity for learning is … that it permits storing far more experiences, far more detailed information about the environment, than can be transmitted in the DNA of the fertilized zygon,' writes Mayr. 'If it is to survive in a constantly changing environment, a bird cannot rely exclusively on the genome. There are far too many gaps in this network of information,' claims Jürgen Nicolai, a scholar of birdsong.[18]

An individual animal learns a surprisingly large proportion of its behavior from its parents, other members of its group, and its environment. The more complex animals become, the more of their behavior is socially or culturally learned. Baby eagles can fly at birth, but their parents must teach them how to land. Teaching is necessary for buffalo to find their mothers in the herd, for reindeer to learn their routes of migration, and for apes to communicate with one another. The significant point here is that, even though genetics can explain the *need* for social learning, once social learning is introduced it brings with it its own evolutionary dynamic, a dynamic that cannot be conceptualized in genetic terms alone.

The irreducibility of culture seems to undercut reductionist views of biology. Our second example involves mentality. Scientists are finding increasing evidence that some of the great apes have a 'theory of other minds'; that is, that they are consciously aware not only of how they see the world but how other animals see the world as well. Animals with even a primitive theory of other minds are able to carry out more complex actions, because they can form inner mental representations that include the perspectives of *other animals* in some situations. Obviously, as soon as this happens, these mental images and intentions become essential for explaining the animals' actions.

Consider a case of deceptive behavior observed and reported by the primatologist Byrne.[19] Byrne observed a young baboon (call him Li'l Al) deceiving his mother into attacking another baboon (call him Big Ted) so that Al could get access to Ted's food. Li'l Al was standing near Ted and hungrily watching him eat a piece of root. Al began making the vocalizations that chimps make when they have been attacked and hurt. His mother quickly spun around and concluded (as Al had hoped she would!) that Big Ted had just attacked her son. She chased him off angrily, whereupon Li'l Al was able to pick up the abandoned piece of root and begin eating it without danger.

Now consider the mental picture that Li'l Al must have formed in order to plan and execute this deceptive action. He had to realize that when he yelped with pain his mother would spin around, and he had to know that *from her perspective* it would look as if Big Ted had just attacked him. Given what his mother would *think* she saw, it would be likely that she would attack Ted and drive him away. Of course, Li'l Al could only plan the deception if he could imagine the world from his mother's perspective and know what she was likely to do given what she *thought* she had just seen. In order to understand and explain these mental intentions and operations, the researcher has to avail herself of some of the notions and explanatory categories that we use in human psychology.

The limits of biological explanation become even clearer when one comes to more complex human behaviors. Only humans, as far as we know, act on the basis of long-term, often highly abstract, self-conscious intentions. For example, imagine you recognize that your habit of eating your roommate's food out of the refrigerator irritates him, and you see that the results of your roommate's irritation tend to be negative for you. So far you haven't shown any cognitive capacities that a chimpanzee couldn't manifest as well. But that's only the start. You then form a self-conscious intention to change your behavior. You develop a complex plan, which includes buying more food, buying it on a more regular basis, and going out to eat when you run out of food. You become aware that your pattern goes back to your early years of living with your parents, who engaged in subtle forms of psychological domination over you, making you feel guilty about physical pleasures. Now you begin to realize that both you and they played a role in developing these patterns, patterns that you are only now bringing to conscious awareness and starting to evaluate. Perhaps you resolve to go into therapy so that you won't be so dominated by the anxieties produced by these early childhood experiences with your parents. You also begin to think of these lifestyle patterns as an ethical issue. Let us imagine that you come to hold the moral belief that it is wrong for you to live off of others in this way.

But you are capable of going even further. You then reflect on *why* your behavior might be wrong. You reject the view that it is wrong only because it leads to bad consequences for you (the view that philosophers call ethical utilitarianism). You recognize, perhaps, that if *all* persons acted according to the maxim, 'Eat other people's food any time you wish,' the cooperation necessary for human social community would become impossible (for instance, no one would want to be anyone else's roommate!). You remember Thomas Hobbes' argument from your freshman philosophy class: behaviors of this kind might lead to 'the war of all against all,' such that life would become 'nasty, brutish, and short.' Upon reflection, you find yourself more drawn to Kant's position: the example reveals a 'categorical imperative,' which lies at the root of all human morality. In the end, you begin to speculate on whether Kant's introduction of God as a regulative condition for moral discourse is sufficient, or whether a God must really exist as the basis for our sense of ethical obligation.

Let me stop you before you become too lost in these lofty speculations, since the point should now be sufficiently clear. *Very, very little of this process can be accounted for in biological terms.* The theoretical concepts you have introduced may or may not prove the existence of a Freudian unconscious, objective moral obligation, or an omnipotent God. However, they do offer fairly strong evidence that human actions are frequently based on psychological and theoretical intentions, and on *meta*-intentions (intentions about what one should intend), and on meta-reflections on those intentions, and on meta–meta-justifications of one's own reflections on one's intentions … and so on.

Our thought experiment seems to have unearthed at least *three* explanatory levels beyond biology, and perhaps many more. First we discovered the non-reducibility of cultural explanations; then we encountered the importance of explanations based on conscious intentions; and finally we saw the natural way in which philosophical reasoning grows out of everyday situations. To discover that *even one* of these levels wasn't reducible to biology, even in principle, would undercut the argument that biology excludes religion. To discover that *all three* of them are essential shows that there are explanatory levels that rise beyond biology. In either case, Dawkins' reductionist assumption is undercut.

WHERE DOES THE DEBATE LEAVE US?

Recall that Dawkins' basic argument against religion ran something like this: such great complexity as we find in the world could only have been created by something equally as complex as the world. For instance, he argues in *The Blind Watchmaker* that 'any God capable of intelligently designing something as complex as the DNA/protein replicating machine itself must have been at least as complex and organized as that machine itself.'[20] Then, he tells us, there are only two options: God is *not* complex enough, so the idea of God cannot account for the complex universe we find. Or, if God *were* complex enough, we would be left with the question, where did *God* come from?

Dawkins tells his readers that there is only one possible answer to his criticisms: 'You [religious believers] have to say something like "God was always there," and if you allow yourself that kind of lazy way out, you might as well say "DNA was always there," or "Life was always there," and be done with it.'[21] As a matter of fact, theists have developed some rather sophisticated accounts of how complex an infinite being would have to be and why it would not itself need a source.

One also finds among religious authors a wide variety of understandings of God. Some view God as including the natural world within the divine being (panentheism). Some reject miracles, construing divine action as another name for the laws of nature. The British philosopher Samuel Alexander treated God or 'divinity' as an emergent property of the natural world itself.

The most famous atheist of the first half of the twentieth century, Bertrand Russell, used science in his famous argument, 'Why I Am Not a Christian.' At the end of his book, *Science and Religion*, he did however affirm a sort of mysticism in response to the cosmos. Albert Einstein picked up on that mystical attitude in his well-known argument for the complementarity of religion and science: 'Science without religion is lame, religion without science is blind.' The British mathematician and logician Alfred North Whitehead wrote:

> Religion is the vision of something which stands beyond, behind, and within, the passing flux of immediate things; something which is real, and yet waiting to be realized; something which is a remote possibility, and yet the greatest of present facts; something that gives meaning to all that passes, and yet eludes apprehension; something whose possession is the final good, and yet is beyond all reach; something which is the ultimate ideal, and the hopeless quest.[22]

No matter which side of the debate one finally comes down on, one might be disappointed that Dawkins does not consider (or even mention) the more sophisticated religious responses. He seems to have dismissed all serious concepts of God, including many that theologians and intelligent religious persons actually hold, leaving only 'lazy' ideas of God. And, as we will see in the next chapter, the number of beliefs about the nature of the ultimate only increases when one looks beyond the framework of the Christian religion.

QUESTIONS FOR REFLECTION AND DISCUSSION

1. Of the two positions presented in this chapter (Intelligent Design and the New Atheism), which do you find more convincing, and why? Do you naturally lean toward one or the other?
2. If you do not find yourself convinced by either view, how could the discussion be constructed differently to make room for your own position? What do you find missing? What assumptions do *both* sides make that you would resist? Why would you resist them?
3. Intelligent Design and New Atheism represent two opposite poles in the religion and science discussion. Some call them the two extremes. Why do you think that these two positions have become so popular in recent years? What does their popularity say about the current state of the religion–science discussion? Are these the only two responses that you can imagine? If not, can you list some other ways in which science and religion might be discussed and related?
4. One thing that Intelligent Design and the New Atheism have in common is their reliance on scientific evidence to ground religious claims on the one hand or arguments against religion on the other. To what extent do the results of science influence *your* religious orientation? How much and what kind of evidence would it take to change your beliefs about God (e.g., from theism to atheism or vice versa)?
5. Consider Alfred North Whitehead's quote at the end of the chapter. Suppose you accepted this definition of religion. On this view, how might religion *differ* from science? How might religion be *similar* to science? How might religion *complement* science? Where do you come down in this debate?

SUGGESTIONS FOR FURTHER READING

John D. Barrow and Frank J. Tipler, *The Anthropic Cosmological Principle* (Oxford: Oxford University Press, 1988).

Michael Behe, *Darwin's Black Box* (New York: Free Press, 2006).

Philip Clayton, *Adventures in the Spirit* (Minneapolis: Fortress Press, 2008).

Richard Dawkins, *The God Delusion* (Boston, MA: Houghton Mifflin, 2006).

Richard Dawkins, *Unweaving the Rainbow: Science, Delusion, and the Appetite for Wonder* (Boston, MA: Houghton Mifflin, 1998).

Robert T. Pennock, *Tower of Babel: The Evidence against the New Creationism* (Cambridge, MA: MIT Bradford, 1999).

John Polkinghorne, *Exploring Reality: The Intertwining of Science and Religion* (New Haven, CT: Yale University Press, 2005).

Hugh Ross, *The Creator and the Cosmos: How the Greatest Scientific Discoveries of the Century Reveal God*, 3rd expanded edn (Colorado Springs, CO: NavPress, 2001).

William Dembski and Michael Ruse, eds, *Debating Design: From Darwin to DNA* (Cambridge: Cambridge University Press, 2004).

Alfred North Whitehead, *Science and the Modern World* (New York: Free Press, 1967).

SCIENCE AND THE WORLD'S RELIGIONS

In the newspapers and textbooks one usually reads about 'religion' and science. Advocates defend religion; its opponents attack it. Both sides tend to assume that there is an essence, a single viewpoint, 'religion,' which either is or is not compatible with science. But *is* there such a thing as 'religion'?

The goal of this chapter is to bring to light the very different kinds of concerns that are raised across the world's religious traditions. The order of presentation is particularly important here. Most readers in the West will implicitly have Christianity in mind when they begin reading a text on religion and science. A particular group of recurring topics tends to set the agenda for debates about Christianity and science: an initial creation 'out of nothing' by God; the purpose or directionality to evolution; human uniqueness and the existence of the soul; the question of miracles; the bodily resurrection of Jesus Christ; the possibility of divine revelation; and the Christian concern with signs of the 'eschaton' (the Second Coming of Christ, which is said to bring about the transition from this order to the next). Perceptive readers will recognize that something similar to this set of issues formed the backdrop for the previous two chapters; it determined the framework for the sometimes harsh debates that we examined there.

But what about religions other than Christianity? It turns out that radically different concerns arise when other religions enter into dialogue with science. In many cases, the relationships with science that emerge are not nearly as conflicted as the ones we have observed so far. This helps explain the frustration that members of other traditions frequently voice about Western books on religion and science:

You are preoccupied with a very peculiar list of Christian concerns. When you encounter conflict with science, you mark all religions with the same branding iron and dismiss them all as a result. But this approach is both inaccurate and unfair. Why don't you study our traditions in their own light, and not just in the shadow of Christianity?

Let us spend some time, then, with each tradition separately. We commence with Judaism, in order to show how vastly different from Christianity are the concerns of historical Jewish thought and of contemporary Jewish thinkers. We then move on to Islam and two of the major Eastern traditions.

JUDAISM

Those who are aware of the way in which the discussion between Christians and science has gone will be immediately struck by the vastly different world of Jewish thought and observance. The Christian questions – at least those which are covered in the media today – often involve sharp oppositions: how can miracles occur? How can a man be raised from the dead? How can the Bible be inerrant in its historical and (implicit) scientific claims? How can God create the world in six days? How can God guide all of history toward His intended goals? How is one to understand the Second Coming of Christ, the judgment, and the establishing of a 'new heaven and a new earth'?

With a few exceptions, to which we will return, the Jewish discussion with science has been very different. For centuries most rabbinical commentators have not worried about the exact historical details about how the text of the Torah arose, nor have they worried whether it is exactly correct on all scientific and historical details. Because obedience of the Law is central to Jewish identity, interpreting the legal requirements was viewed as more urgent, since the primary task of the rabbis was to guide Jews in their religious observance.

Specific events in the history of the Jewish people further influenced Jewish thinking. The second destruction of the Temple in CE 70 led Jewish scholars to interpret specific predictions and prophecies in the Hebrew Bible more metaphorically and less historically. God's calling to his chosen people was obviously broader than maintaining the Temple cult, which is what a literal reading of the Torah would have led one to expect. Moreover, the concerns of a people in diaspora, with no homeland and often fighting for survival in the face of persecution, were more pressing and more concrete. The Shoah (or Holocaust) in the twentieth century raised very fundamental questions about God's presence and care for Jews, questions that could not be answered by a literal reading of the Tanakh (the Jewish Bible) alone.

Now add to all these factors the incredible influence of Maimonides (1135–1204) and the tradition of 'negative theology' – a tradition extended into the Jewish mystical or 'Kabbalistic' tradition. The net result was a very different understanding of those theological debates that don't directly bear on observance. Among Jewish commentators, one finds a widespread willingness to treat many claims in the Hebrew Bible as metaphorical or figurative: the six days of creation, concrete historical claims, divine miracles, and details that might otherwise resemble scientific claims. There are even passages in rabbinical commentary (*midrash*) which suggest that rabbis should be guided by the best (i.e., most reasonable) interpretation of the Torah even over what might appear to be a direct sign from God. It doesn't take much reflection to realize that this attitude will produce a very different sort of religion–science debate than one finds in the books by the best-known Christian thinkers.

Judaism is a minority religion in almost all of the countries of the world. The number of observant Jews is also declining in most countries. Among the many reasons are the facts that Judaism is not a proselytizing religion; one has to be born of a Jewish mother to be Jewish, and observance of the Law is demanding and often inconvenient. Given this decline, it is a matter of great Jewish concern that observant couples who want to have children are able to do so. This fact has led Jewish scholars and scientists to take a strong interest in fertility treatments and in genetic studies that might reduce the incidence of genetic diseases. Arguably, the rich tradition of interpreting the Torah and the commentaries on the Torah, and the value placed on study as contributing to Jewish identity and practice, have given ethics a particularly important place in Jewish thought and practice.

These factors, though presented here only in the briefest outline, help explain some of the distinctively Jewish emphases in the religion–science debate. Consider these three. First, Jewish thinkers have generally been welcoming of, rather than resistant to, new scientific breakthroughs in fundamental physics, cosmology, origins of life research, evolutionary biology, and ecology.[1] Overall, one encounters little anxiety or defensiveness about science in general or about new scientific theories. When Jewish authors relate scientific theories to the Tanakh, the Jewish Bible, they tend to write comfortably about how the results are consistent with Jewish identity. Analogies are drawn with teachings in the Torah and *midrash*, and writers tend to draw positive parallels for Jewish thought, identity, and practice. In reading these works, you generally don't detect the worry that Jews face a bunch of dangerous conceptual conflicts that must be overcome.

Second, ethical and political questions often move to the forefront; they tend to be far more important than the question of how Jewish beliefs could be true in light of science. For most Jewish scholars and educated readers, the more interesting questions lie elsewhere: how are humans different from other animals? What is distinctive about human existence? Are humans basically selfish rather than altruistic? Are we primarily individualistic or social? When are genetic interventions allowed, and when are they wrong? Could scientists someday build a robot that would be indistinguishable from biological persons?

When scientific results seem to show why Jewish observance is healthy or rational or functional, they naturally receive more positive attention; results that seem to undercut Jewish practices are reviewed with concern (and sometimes dismissiveness). Jewish authors have written some of the best analyses of the ethics of scientific research and practice, and their subtle and complex analyses often set the standard for other authors.[2] Finally, another tradition of Jewish writing offers more mystical readings of the scientific results. Where this tradition predominates, science is generally used as a means for emphasizing the spiritual connection humans can have with the universe and with its Creator.[3]

The third and final area concerns the responses of Orthodox Jewish thinkers. Here a different set of concerns comes to the fore. Consider three examples. The Orthodox biologist Carl Feit at

Yeshiva University grapples with the apparently reductive implications of contemporary genetics.[4] Cyril Domb, like some Orthodox thinkers, tries to reconcile a more literal reading of Genesis with contemporary scientific evidence, in a fashion that many Christian and Muslim readers will find familiar.[5] Finally, the biologist Robert Pollack at Columbia University argues for a sharp separation between the results of science and Jewish belief and practice. He resists efforts to integrate the two and argues that they belong to sharply separate realms.[6]

Authors from all the major Jewish denominations – Orthodox, Conservative, and Reform – have great concern for the nation of Israel. For many Jews, Zionism is not just a political question but a deeply religious conviction as well. Books that suggest a historical or archeological basis for the early occupation of Palestine by the Israelites attract great attention in Israel, as do archeological data that might help in dating the first or second destruction of the Temple or providing details about its construction.

There is one final feature about Judaism and science that distinguishes it from Christianity–science dialogues: the capacity to disagree with grace. Rabbis have always disagreed about virtually every topic they have written about, so Jewish scholars don't expect a convergence of opinion. Early in my career I remember watching three Jewish scholars dispute over science–religion topics and thinking, 'They'll never talk to each other again after this battle!' Yet when the Friday afternoon session ended, the three scholars donned their coats and prepared to walk to the synagogue together for the opening of *Shabbat*. Christians have much to learn from this capacity to disagree gracefully.

ISLAM

Islam was one of the first traditions to engage 'natural philosophy,' the predecessor to modern science. Muslim philosophers first translated Aristotle's writings into Arabic, which led to their translation into Latin and their growing influence in the West. But until recently the dialogue between Islam and modern science seemed to be a far lower priority.

In the past few years, however, the discussion has begun to receive intense attention. It is far more multifaceted than most readers realize. Some thinkers mirror the oppositional language of the more conservative wings of the Christianity–science debate; others call for a smooth integration of Islam and contemporary science; and others describe Islam as the 'bridge' between the Western theistic traditions and the more mystical traditions of the East.

Seyyed Hossein Nasr speaks for many Muslims, both in the Arab world and in the West, when he challenges the identification of all science with Western science and calls for a distinctively 'Islamic Science.' Materialism, naturalism, and reductionism – in short, a worldview hostile to God – have come to dominate contemporary science. Looking back to the medieval writings on nature by Jewish, Muslim, and Christian authors, these authors argue that it is not necessary for science to be anti-religious. Thus Muslims (and, by implication, other theists) should develop and practice forms of science that do without these assumptions:

> Any science that could legitimately be called Islamic science, and not be disruptive of the whole Islamic order, must be one that remains aware of the 'vertical cause' of all things, along with the horizontal, a science that issues from and returns to the Real (*al-Haqq*), Who is the Cause of all things.[7]

Reductionism and materialism are not intrinsic features of science; they are unfortunate by-products of decoupling the pursuit of knowledge from the search for wisdom. We should look first for signs (*āyāt*) of the Creator's hand in the world around us. Once we have the correct metaphysics in place, it is unproblematic to develop specific scientific theories and technologies. But if we do not first acknowledge God, they argue science will end up working in opposition to the Creator of all things – and thereby fall eventually into falsehood.[8]

Defenders of Islamic science focus on a close reading of the Qur'an as a guide for knowing when science has drawn correct conclusions and when it errs (or goes beyond the evidence) and begins to manifest materialist and anti-theological prejudices. Like the secular 'cultural critics,' these authors call for a recognition of political biases – in particular, Western imperialist interests – in the allegedly neutral scientific theories. Western science promotes

Western interests. When these are recognized, they argue, it becomes possible to develop forms of science that can promote the insights of Islam.

What kinds of questions interest Islamic writers and readers? Distinctive themes include the dependence of all knowledge and truth on God; the order in nature as reflecting God's creative activity; the need to begin with an initial divine creation in order to account for the world as we see it; the uniqueness of human beings in comparison to the animals; questions about what is the essence of humanity; the purposiveness of creation; the teleology or directedness of evolution, and hence the general preference for Intelligent Design over Darwinian biology (see Chapter 2). Authors describe the essence of human beings as moral and religious beings, looking to both science and revelation to understand what are our moral and religious obligations. One frequently reads lists of signs (āyāt) that the universe is meant to run according to principles of justice, along with discussions of what those principles are. Muslim authors sometimes explore evidence that God is directing the entire process toward some particular outcome, including signs of divine judgment. History-based (and sometimes science-based) arguments are offered for the uniqueness of Islam and its superiority to other religions. Similar to the Jewish case, Muslim authors also look for scientific evidence that Islamic law (sharia) is conducive to human health and happiness.

Some Muslim authors hold that it is sufficient to study the Qur'an, Hadīth (the words and deeds of the prophet Mohammed), and Sharia. But many thinkers also emphasize the study of philosophy as an important means for expanding beyond narrow views of science. If metaphysical language is dismissed as meaningless, how can one possibly recognize the role of the Creator? Thus, Nasr writes,

> Modern science must be studied in its philosophical foundations from the Islamic point of view, in order to reveal for Muslims exactly what the value system is upon which [science] is based and how this value system opposes, complements, or threatens the Islamic value system.[9]

Muslims believe almost universally that the Qur'an was dictated by Allah and his prophet Mohammed, so that the Arabic text thus expresses a direct communication by God. Many equate being a Muslim with regarding the Qur'an as the literal words of God. Nevertheless, there are an increasing number of Muslim thinkers who argue for the necessity of developing a Muslim hermeneutic, that is, principles for interpreting the Qur'anic texts in light of science and philosophy.

An important new book by Nidhal Guessoum, *Islam's Quantum Question: Reconciling Muslim Tradition and Modern Science*,[10] argues for the possibility that there can be multiple readings and interpretations of some of the Qur'an's passages. Sometimes the best interpretation is not literal but allegorical. The principles for allegorical interpretation can be traced back to the great medieval Islamic philosopher Ibn Rushd (Averroes). When there appears to be a contradiction, 'the (religious) Text must be allegorically understood and subjected to interpretation by those whom the Qur'an calls "rooted in knowledge."' Reclaiming these classic Islamic ideas would greatly reduce the tension between Islam and contemporary science. If it is accepted,

> one [could] convince the Muslim public of a given idea (say the theory of biological evolution), not by proving that it can be found in the Qur'an but rather by showing that at least one intelligent reading and interpretation of its verses is fully consistent with the scientific theory in question.[11]

Some Muslim thinkers go even further. A movement known as 'progressive Muslims' is seeking to develop a 'critical-progressive Islamic hermeneutics.'[12] One can also find more radically secularist readings of Islam and science. Rather than sharing Guessoum's attempt to reconcile the core of Islam with science, these Muslim thinkers argue for a more liberal form of Islam that can fit within the parameters of contemporary science. The Turkish Muslim philosopher Taner Edis, for example, opposes the 'Islamizing' of science. He writes:

> The best way to achieve Muslim harmony with science might be to promote liberal tendencies within Islam.... [The moderate Muslim intellectuals] think of Islam as a godly and yet sophisticated civilization rather than a rigid set of divinely ordained rules

of conduct.... They perceive a meaning in the universe that transcends mere material goings-on without contradicting scientific statements about subatomic particles or the evolution of frogs.[13]

We close with two interesting features of the recent Islam–science discussion. One dimension involves the growing environmental movement among Muslims, including a rich use of the Islamic tradition to foster ecological awareness and concern.[14] The other stems from the long Muslim tradition of mysticism and negative theology, which influences many Muslim responses to science. Sufi mystics have traditionally emphasized the unknowability of God, holding that one can only experience God through nature, other human beings, and mystical experience. Sufi authors beautifully and poetically evoke the divine in and through nature, encouraging spiritual rather than literal interpretations of contemporary science and its conclusions. One can trace this emphasis on God in and through all things all the way back to the thirteenth-century mystic Ibn 'Arabī. Perhaps you can hear something of this approach in the words of the French astrophysicist and Muslim Bruno Guiderdoni:

> I would like to protect religion from [the] kind of misunderstanding where religion is submitted to the approval of scientists or the judgment of science. There is [a] whole dimension of spiritual life that is completely neglected by this scientific approach that is just interested in 'scientific facts.' We are not looking for facts in religion. We are looking for our inner transformation, for the improvement of our societies, and for the fruits which will come, *insha' Allah*, in the Hereafter.[15]

Clearly these more mystical Islamic voices offer a path to a less conflictual relationship with contemporary science than one sees in thinkers like Nasr. They also evidence important connections with some of the Eastern traditions, to which we now turn.

HINDUISM

Hindu thinkers have been at the forefront of religion–science discussion in several respects. One contribution has been to emphasize common features that run across the world's traditions. Gandhi famously praised Jesus as an important spiritual teacher and identified with some core Christian positions. (He is reported to have said, 'I like your Christ, I do not like your Christians. Your Christians are so unlike your Christ.') Many Hindu thinkers like to cite the text from the Gospel of John, 'The kingdom of God is within you.' Deepak Chopra concludes,

> Christ-consciousness, God-consciousness, Krishna-consciousness, Buddha-consciousness – it's all the same thing. Rather than 'Love thy neighbor,' this consciousness says, 'You and I are the same beings.'

This Hindu emphasis tends to raise attention above the specific doctrinal (historical, philosophical) claims defended by the different religions and to concentrate attention instead on what they share in common. When one moves to this level, many of the specific conflicts with science decrease in importance.

What is it in the Hindu tradition that encourages this approach? Hinduism began as a series of sacred practices based on the Vedas, extremely ancient sacred texts which were mostly focused on carrying out specific rituals and healings. The Vedas spoke of the activity of a very large number of gods, of their natures, and of the appropriate forms of devotion required of believers. But in the centuries that followed, deep philosophical reflection on these gods and practices gave rise to the highly rarified religious and philosophical system known as Vedanta. These reflections are contained in the Upanishads, which are among the most sacred scriptures of Hinduism, and in later writings. The Upanishads still speak of numerous gods, but they tend to relativize the gods as manifestations of a single ultimate reality, Brahman. The world of appearance and change is also relativized; it becomes *maya*, illusion. (Whether it is a total illusion, or only a lower level of reality in comparison to Brahman, remains a matter of intense debate.)

This more philosophical form of Hinduism leads to a very different sort of religion–science discussion. It accounts for the more mystical approach of many Hindu writers. The world can be accepted in its various forms of manifestation, and it can be studied by scientists without any conflict, but Hindu thinkers will generally insist that, ultimately, all these phenomena are manifestations of one single ultimate reality. All living things are contained within Brahman and express its nature in one way or another. Regularities in physical movement – what scientists call natural laws – are manifestations of the will and the habits of Brahman. Understood in this way, Hindu belief does not seem to come into significant conflict with the sciences.

It does, however, lead to a particular focus: the study of consciousness. Brahman exists in an eternal and unchanging state of existence, consciousness, and bliss (*satchidananda*, or *Sat-cit-ānanda*). According to the great mystical philosopher Sankara, whose writings are at the center of the 'non-dual' (*advaita*) tradition in Hinduism, these are the only three qualities that Brahman possesses; it is otherwise wholly without attributes (*nirguna Brahman*). As a result, we can know ultimate reality only through blissful awareness, which means only through our own meditation and consciousness. This has led Hindu thinkers to study the evolution and functioning of consciousness with the same sort of intensity that Buddhist thinkers have (as we will see in a moment).

Since there is only the one Brahman and all things are part of it, Hindu scholars have usually resisted any ultimate dualism of mind and body. This has made them interested in studying the ways in which mind–body connections work in human existence. They have generally been integrationists and interactionists, advocating a holistic approach to the human person. (We return to traditional Indian medicine shortly.) But there is also a deeper reason for the focus on consciousness, one that can lead to some conflict with contemporary science. The Upanishads also affirm that there is an eternal principle in each living thing, a soul or Ātman. It is this Ātman that is reincarnated again and again through the cycle of birth and rebirth (*samsara*). Hindu practice and thought exists for the ultimate purpose of liberation from this cycle (*nirvana*). Thus many Hindu scholars hope that the empirical study of consciousness will shed some light on the nature of this ultimate metaphysical principle, Ātman. This focus on an eternal soul has led to some conflict with Western scientists and their approaches to the study of the human person.

The conservative wing in the Hinduism–science discussion exhibits certain parallels with the conservatives in the Christian and

Muslim traditions. Perhaps its most extreme form is manifested in those thinkers who maintain that all the major scientific discoveries of the modern period are already present in the Vedas, the original Hindu scriptures. This school defends the superiority of Hinduism over other traditions, highlighting science that supports core tenets of Hindu thought and challenging scientific results that appear to be opposed to them.

Mainstream Hindu thought does not make these claims. In some religions devotees are unlikely to be practicing scientists, but one often encounters Hindu practitioners who are physicists, engineers, neuroscientists, or doctors. As a Hindu physicist once told me, 'Scratch a scientist in India, and you are likely to find a deeply devout spiritual person.' They experience no tension between their science and their spiritual practices: keeping an altar in the home, bringing offerings to temples, and practicing the traditional ceremonies. Hindu belief and practice are likely to affect their ethical judgments, their beliefs about what is morally right and wrong, and their political stances on the burning issues in Indian politics today.

Outsiders sometimes find it difficult at first to work their way into Hindu writings on science and spirituality. Texts include the ancient Sanskrit terms and details of Vedantic metaphysics; contemporary topics are often explained in terms of the six classical philosophical schools of India; and scientific details are interspersed with narratives from the Vedas, the Upanishads, and the Bhagavad Gita. But one quickly comes to recognize the deep sense of spiritual connection that lies beneath and fuels the traditional accounts. The metaphysical details and stories of gods are meant not as ends but as means to direct the meditator's attention beyond appearances (*maya*) to the ultimate unity of all things.

Writings on Hinduism and modern science have been dominated by a very different set of concerns than one finds in the Abrahamic faiths. In first place comes the study of the nature and efficacy of consciousness. In quantum physics, in evolutionary biology and ecosystem studies, in medicine and all aspects of human studies, Hindu scholars have sought to show that consciousness plays an indispensable role in the functioning of the universe. Purely materialistic explanations cannot be sufficient.

This same commitment motivates extensive work on mind–body connections. Hindu authors invariably seek to reveal the mental or spiritual dimensions in the phenomena that scientists (one-sidedly) study. They list scientific results that show the possibility of enhancing human potential through yogic and other practices. Traditional Indian medicine, or *ayurveda* (the 'science of life') seeks to restore the balance of mind and body. Treatment is holistic; it involves herbal remedies and other medical techniques, but also meditation, mantras, and rites of purification. Because all persons are composites of *prakṛti* and *purusa*, or (roughly) fundamental matter and pure consciousness, medical science must learn to address both sides of human existence. Two specialists, Agrawal and Tiwari, write,

> Today, Ayurveda is increasingly popular because it speaks of those elementary concepts of (1) contact with nature, (2) holism, and (3) we are what we eat.... Its principles are utilized, not only to treat individuals who are ill, but also to prepare balanced meals and construct harmonious environments. Ayurveda brings to life the concepts of preventive health care and health promotion. The ultimate goal of Ayurveda is to help the individual discover a personal knowledge of living.[16]

Admittedly, there are also strands of Hindu thought that are somewhat harder to synthesize with the attitudes and results of Western science. Some authors seek empirical demonstration of the super- and paranormal abilities of the most advanced yogis. Books and conversations in India include accounts of their abilities to levitate, to stop their breathing, to survive without food or oxygen, and to recall experiences from one or more past lives. These are taken as empirical, even 'scientific' evidence that the doctrines of karma and reincarnation are true.

Still, Hindu scholars across the sciences are less known for these proofs and more for their emphasis on the mystical dimension of reality. The mathematical order and lawfulness of the physical universe, they argue, can and should prompt a deep spiritual response. Authors frequently encourage readers to discern the Ātman in plants and animals throughout the biosphere. Physiology, neurology, and medicine need to be pursued not 'mechanically' but with an awareness of the spiritual dimensions of human existence. Above all else, Hindus emphasize the oneness of all reality in, or as,

Brahman. They encourage meditation and spiritual reflection on science, with the goal of realizing the ultimately mental nature of all existing things as manifestations of a single reality and experiencing the connection of all existing things.[17]

Thus, for example, the Indian physicist George Sudarshan writes, 'In the Hindu tradition ... the spiritual quest is in fact not distinct from the scientific, aesthetic or, for that matter, any academic pursuit.' He adds,

> In my own life, I have been privileged to experience the joy and ecstasy of discovery in both the scientific and spiritual domains. In such moments, the distinction between scientific and spiritual paths vanishes for me. In fact, the feeling is identical for both.

To support this view, Sudarshan appeals to a set of spiritual beliefs and practices:

> The Hinduism of Central and South Asia believes instead that God manifests Himself, or Herself, in many ways and in many contexts. My tradition affirms that any spiritual search, whether academic or not, is bound to lead to God. Within Hinduism, there is nothing which is not sacred. God is not an isolated event, something separate from the universe. God is the universe.[18]

BUDDHISM

Buddhism is widely regarded as the easiest religion to synthesize with contemporary science.[19] One could argue whether this reflects a permanent feature of Buddhism or whether it signals how much Buddhist belief and practice has successfully adapted to the modern scientific world, at least in the West. Still, the outcome is the same in either case: Buddhist belief and practice today has become the poster child for successfully integrating religion and science.

Especially in comparison with Christianity and Islam, Buddhism – or at least Western Buddhism – seems to have slid into the scientific age with surprisingly little friction, conflict, or disharmony. Buddhist thinkers and practitioners frequently emphasize that this religion (if they still consider it to be a religion) focuses on meditation; it is primarily a way of seeing the world and a mode of existing in the world. They admit that Tibetan Buddhists and Japanese PureLand Buddhists (to name just two examples) held and continue to hold a wide variety of very specific religious and metaphysical beliefs. But the spokespersons for Buddhism in the West today tend to place the focus on meditative practices rather than demanding strict adherence to traditional beliefs. (Scholars dispute whether this approach reflects the core of the Buddhist stance or rather a smart and creative move on the part of its best-known teachers.) Thus, for example, the Dalai Lama has famously proclaimed that, if contemporary science conflicts with any tenets of Tibetan Buddhism, he will side with science and against the tradition.[20]

In some ways, this 'minimalist' Buddhist approach is not unlike the mystical Hindu approach that we encountered above, but its metaphysical sparseness is probably unmatched across the world's traditions. The 'minimalist' Buddhist practitioner engages in a variety of meditative practices. She holds certain values about living with and treating other living things. At most, she will espouse some very general metaphysical beliefs (though she may not think of them as metaphysical at all!), such as the belief that all things are interrelated or interdependent, or that all that exists is 'inter-being.'[21] She may or may not affirm the traditional doctrine of reincarnation.

If you have participated in these sorts of dialogues you will know that this minimalism can produce a sometimes humorous dynamic in dialogues with scientists. Scientists are used to interactions with Christians or Muslims, who may challenge core tenets of scientific method or express metaphysical beliefs that stand in some significant tension with accepted scientific laws. In dialogue with Western Buddhists, by contrast, he is initially surprised to find them emphasizing that there can be no possible conflict between Buddhism and science. He senses that his Buddhist discussion partners hold some beliefs that don't exactly jive with the way contemporary science approaches the questions, but he has trouble putting his finger on exactly where the differences lie. At conferences this leads to some amusing exchanges, in which the scientists say, 'Well, surely you must believe something more than that.

Surely "inter-being" and "Dependent Arising" are metaphysical assertions for which one will need some evidence.' And the Western Buddhists will often reply, 'No, we're not making any metaphysical claims at all. Our words are only expressions of our feelings about existence, or subjective impressions that arise during meditation. So there is no possible conflict and no need for metaphysical justifications.' 'But surely you're making some metaphysical claims.' 'No, we aren't!' 'Yes, you are!'

It is harder than you would think to resolve this debate. It does seem strange for a scientist to tell a religious person that they are *too* minimalist and that they *ought* to hold more robust metaphysical beliefs, beliefs that would conflict more dramatically with science! After all, many scientists have been calling on the religious traditions to reinterpret their beliefs so that they become guidelines for ethics and spiritual practices rather than metaphysical (or, worse, scientific) claims. Many of these same scientists point to Buddhism as an ideal and example in this regard.[22]

But on one point the skeptic is probably right: for Buddhism the world is not a value-free natural system. Both as a whole and in every part, the natural world is shot through with value. The reason is not because it is created by a transcendent God – for Buddhists, it isn't – but because the Buddha taught that everything is of value just as it is and for being what it is. Meditation and Buddhist practice are not about escaping from the world but about developing a deeper practice of compassion for all living things because of what they most truly are, each possessing its own unique value. One sees this reflected in the poem, 'Dewdrops on a Lotus Leaf,' by the famous Zen Buddhist author Ryokan (1758–1831):

> The wind has settled, the blossoms have fallen;
> Birds sing, the mountains grow dark –
> This is the wondrous power of Buddhism.

The Enlightened one perceives the infinite value of each individual precisely because there *is* no other reality or ground or transcendent source except the one reality that exists.

The result is a comprehensive and rather demanding ethic, one that presupposes a world suffused with values. Yet doesn't this picture of the world stand at some distance from the naturalized, value-free picture of the world that today's natural sciences paint? It certainly seems to be a far cry from the reductionist drive of science, with its attempt to explain all phenomena in terms of their most basic constituents and laws. Indeed, the Buddhist worldview is the opposite of reductionism, since it affirms the full and irreducible value of every manifestation of life in the universe, of every life form, no matter what its evolutionary history or level of complexity. Moreover, it places great value on the phenomenon of consciousness or awareness, which – at least in the forms in which human beings experience it – is an extreme latecomer in the field of evolution.

This difference leads us to one of the really distinct features of the science-and-Buddhism dialogue: the focus on consciousness. Buddhist scholars are very strongly motivated to engage in the study of consciousness, its origins, and its effects. They do not have any compulsion to link consciousness with some immaterial soul that carries and produces it. As a result, they are extremely interested in studying the natural emergence of consciousness, its evolution, its manifestations in humans and other animals, its contents, and its effects. *That* in turn inclines Buddhists to be allies with scientists across the whole range of sciences that bear on consciousness: the human sciences, of course, but also cognitive science, neuroscience, evolutionary psychology, genetics, and the classical Darwinian accounts of evolutionary history. If one is only interested in how consciousness arises and what its dynamics are, one need not fear or resist results of any of these disciplines, for all shed light on that question.

The other Buddhist focus is on the *contents* of consciousness. The technical name for this study is 'phenomenology'; it involves the study of phenomena as they are presented to conscious awareness and as we immediately experience them. Buddhist focus on lived experience has actually helped to produce a new area of cooperation between scientists and Buddhists that many take to be a model for science–religion work to come. Known as the study of the 'neural correlates of consciousness,' this approach focuses on the correlations between perceived conscious states and brain activity. Famous experiments have been carried out (among others) by Richard Davidson and his team at the University of Wisconsin – studies that were directly supported by the Dalai Lama, who asked some of his closest monks to participate and who personally toured the research facility. The monk being studied, drawing on thousands of hours of religious practice, would place himself in a meditative state, engaging, for example, in Compassion meditation. Changes in his brain state were measured using real-time brain-imaging techniques such as fMRI scans. Specific stimuli were then applied, such as sounding a loud noise near his ears or lightly prick-ing his skin with a pin. The brain responses were measured and then contrasted with the responses of the same subject when not meditating and with the responses of untrained meditators. Davidson found that those with previous training showed greater activity in areas of the brain dedicated to paying attention and making decisions.

What makes these results particularly interesting is that the scientific data produced *could not have be acquired without reference to the mental or conscious state that the subject was in.* This scientific research studies human beings in their full or 'emergent' form; it depends on the conscious awareness and intentions that the subjects themselves produce and experience. Rather than 'reducing' con-sciousness, the experimenters were *presupposing* consciousness. Put differently, the scientific knowledge was acquired, in part, by means of the religious beliefs and practices of the subject, rather than by asking the researcher to view religious beliefs as mistaken or at least irrelevant.

Scientists may welcome this sort of experimental method because it provides data on how mental experiences and brain states are correlated. For their part, Buddhist thinkers are enthusiastic about scientific evidence which shows that the discipline of medi-tation can actually alter one's perception of the world. Some schol-ars suggest that religion–science discussions should concentrate on partnerships of this kind where there can be satisfaction on both sides, rather than on those areas where religious belief and scientific results stand in dramatic tension.

Of course, Buddhists have not limited themselves to assisting scientists; in other areas they attempt to go beyond the results of science. Numerous Buddhist thinkers have engaged in introspec-tive or 'phenomenological' studies as a means for acquiring know-ledge.[23] B. Alan Wallace, for example, a leading scholar/practitioner of Buddhism and science, is working toward 'a new science of consciousness.'[24] Beyond the realm of natural science 'is a state in which words and concepts are suspended,' a state where theory 'is nothing more than a conceptual overlay.' The final goal of Buddhist practice is not science but 'the overcoming of all the usual barriers between the individual and the ultimate ground of being.'

Of course, the Buddhism-and-science dialogue also has its critics. Some argue that the pro-scientific statements are actually nothing more than good propaganda. Buddhism is, after all, a religious system, and it includes a large number of 'superstitious' beliefs that clash with the scientific mindset. Other critics argue that the focus on the subjective contents of consciousness cannot be scientific, because it is not objectively testable and verifiable. It is fine for Buddhist subjects to participate in scientific experiments as long as the terms of the collaboration are set by the laboratory researchers. But the critics warn against allowing meditative practices (and the convictions they produce) to bypass scientific testing and pass for knowledge of reality. Belief in reincarnation, for example, is basic to all the traditions of Buddhist doctrine and is presupposed in most Buddhist rituals. Yet reincarnation actually presupposes something essential about a person that can continue from life to life. This belief, the critics note, cannot be consistent with any naturalist understanding of the world, and actually flies in the face of what we know about the dependence of 'mind' on states of the brain and body.[25]

CONCLUSIONS AND FURTHER QUESTIONS TO EXPLORE

At the beginning of this chapter I noted that critics frequently allege that religion, *by its very nature*, stands in tension with science. To speak in such generalities, I suggested, does not do justice to the incredible diversity between religious traditions and interests.

Some amazing cultural upheavals are taking place as each of the world's major religious traditions encounters modern science and begins to interact with it. In every case there is change. Some traditions immediately go into battle mode, placing themselves for decades or even centuries in an oppositional stance to most of what contemporary science stands for. They criticize specific results (especially those that conflict with their own traditional beliefs);

they challenge the assumptions that underlie science, such as materialism and naturalism; they interpret science as a worldview and then contrast it to their own beliefs about ultimate reality. These traditions will often offer their own competing form of science in its place, as in Islamic science or various forms of Native American science. Other religions are torn for decades or centuries between 'modernist' and 'traditionalist' schools; one thinks of the intense debate over Modernism that rocked the Catholic Church in the late nineteenth century and continues into the present. Still other traditions such as Buddhism seem to slide effortlessly into the scientific age with little friction or conflict or disharmony.

Studying the various traditions in their distinctness should not obscure common themes across the traditions. Intelligent Design has adherents in Christianity, Islam, and even among some Jews and Hindus. Likewise, 'progressive' or liberal approaches across the traditions share important features in common. Orthodox Jews and conservative Christians sometimes share a common interest in using science to defend the accuracy of the Hebrew Bible, and Muslims have similar interests for the Qur'an. Hindus and Buddhists are interested in evidence from the neurosciences that meditation can change brain states and, in particular, that the neurological responses of advanced meditators are different from the brains of ordinary people.

Certainly the diversity we have encountered in this chapter undercuts the claim that all religions are simply hostile to science. In fact, some will respond, shouldn't other traditions emulate the remarkable harmony that arises (for example) in many discussions of Buddhism and science? Shouldn't one focus on the areas of overlap and compatibility, holding them up as a model for those religious traditions that are caught in a much more volatile relationship with contemporary science? Is it possible that Christianity or Islam could discover a similar harmony? Or is the rejection of science that one sees in many Christian and Muslim authors simply intrinsic to these traditions?

Our exploration suggests one final possibility: that the religions, when one abstracts from their specific beliefs and traditions, may together point toward a more general feature of human existence that we might call 'human spirituality.' The term 'spirituality' connotes experiences of wholeness, integration, timelessness, or meaningfulness that many people report. These experiences may come unbidden to an individual; they may arise as a response to great sadness or inner turmoil; or they may result from disciplined spiritual practices such as meditation or prayer pursued over many years. Why should one say that such spiritual experiences have to stand in tension with the scientific project? After all, in and of themselves they make no knowledge claims. They seem more strongly connected with specific internal states and impressions about human existence as experienced by a particular individual. Or perhaps they are by-products of an inner encounter with God or some deeper dimension of reality.

In this regard, it is interesting to read the comments on spirituality by some of the most vocal science-based opponents of religion, such as Richard Dawkins and Daniel Dennett. Both individuals have commented in public that they know something of spiritual experience; both are happy to call themselves 'spiritual but not religious.' If the most vocal opponents of religion are willing to countenance the spiritual dimension of human existence, how could anyone argue that spirituality (in this sense) and science are intrinsically incompatible? And if they *aren't* incompatible, couldn't one work with the various religious traditions to identify those features of each tradition that focus on this spiritual dimension, which means the features that could be most easily synthesized with the sciences? In such a project, Buddhists will clearly play a leading role, but it could well be that this project could be extended to many other traditions as well. We return to this topic in the final chapter.

QUESTIONS FOR REFLECTION AND DISCUSSION

1. What kinds of factors within a religion promote dialogue with the sciences and a positive attitude toward scientific evidence? Which characteristics tend to produce conflict with science?
2. What do the religions discussed in this chapter have in common with each other? What are some of the areas in which they differ?
3. If you belong to a particular religion, how would you characterize your own tradition's relationship to science? How is this

relationship different from or similar to that of other religions discussed above?

4. Does the harmony (or possible harmony) of Buddhism and science offer a model that other religions could emulate? Are there intrinsic features of the other religions that make it more difficult for them to achieve the same harmony? Or could there be *other forms* of harmony between religion and science that these other traditions could establish?

5. Different religions pose different kinds of questions to science or about the limits of science. Which questions matter most to you, and which matter least? Do you find one religion's set of questions more interesting than another? (Note: it may not be the religion that you belong to or are most familiar with.) Can you name some questions about religion and science that do not arise within *any* of the religions that we have so far discussed?

SUGGESTIONS FOR FURTHER READING

Saleem H. Ali, *Treasures of the Earth: Need, Greed and a Sustainable Future* (New Haven, CT: Yale University Press, 2009).

Jacob Bronowski, *Science and Human Values* (New York: Messner, 1956).

Geoffrey Cantor and Marc Swetlitz, eds, *Jewish Tradition and the Challenge of Darwinism* (Chicago, IL: University of Chicago Press, 2006).

Philip Clayton, ed., *Oxford Handbook of Religion and Science* (Oxford: Oxford University Press, 2006).

Pranab Das, ed., *Global Perspectives on Science and Spirituality* (West Conshohocken, PA: Templeton Press, 2009).

Richard J. Davidson and Anne Harrington, *Visions of Compassion: Western Scientists and Tibetan Buddhists Examine Human Nature* (New York: Oxford University Press, 2001).

Cyril Domb and Aryeh Carmell, eds, *Challenge: Torah Views on Science and its Problems* (London: Association of Orthodox Jewish Scientists; New York: Feldheim, 1976).

Taner Edis, *An Illusion of Harmony: Science and Religion in Islam* (Amherst, NY: Prometheus Books, 2007).

Noah J. Efron, *Judaism and Science: A Historical Introduction* (Westport, CT: Greenwood Press, 2007).

Richard C. Foltz *et al.*, eds, *Islam and Ecology: A Bestowed Trust* (Cambridge, MA: Harvard University Press, 2003).

Mehdi Golshani, *Issues in Islam and Science* (Tehran: Institute for Humanities and Cultural Studies, 2004).

Lenn E. Goodman, *Creation and Evolution* (Abingdon, UK: Routledge, 2010).

Nidhal Guessoum, *Islam's Quantum Question: Reconciling Muslim Tradition and Modern Science* (London: I.B. Tauris, 2011).

Thich Nhat Hanh, *Interbeing: Fourteen Guidelines for Engaged Buddhism*, 3rd edn (Berkeley, CA: Parallax Press, 1998); *Understanding Our Mind* (Berkeley, CA: Parallax Press, 2006).

Donald S. Lopez, Jr., *Buddhism and Science: A Guide for the Perplexed* (Chicago, IL: University of Chicago Press, 2008).

Daniel Matt, *God and the Big Bang: Discovering Harmony Between Science and Spirituality* (Woodstock, VT: Jewish Lights Publishing, 1996).

Sangeetha Menon, ed., *Consciousness, Experience, and Ways of Knowing: Perspectives from Science, Philosophy and the Arts* (Bangalore: National Institute of Advanced Studies, 2006).

Ābrahim Özdemir, *The Ethical Dimension of Human Attitude towards Nature: A Muslim Perspective* (Istanbul: Insan Publications, 2008).

Makarand Paranjape, ed., *Science, Spirituality and the Modernization of India* (London: Anthem Press, 2009).

Robert Pollack, *The Faith of Biology and the Biology of Faith: Order, Meaning, and Free Will in Modern Medical Science* (New York: Columbia University Press, 2000).

Joel R. Primack and Nancy Ellen Abrams, *The View from the Center of the Universe: Discovering Our Extraordinary Place in the Cosmos* (New York: Penguin Riverhead, 2006).

Matthieu Ricard and Trinh Xuan Thuan, *The Quantum and the Lotus* (New York: Crown, 2001).

Evan Thompson, *Mind in Life: Biology, Phenomenology, and the Sciences of Mind* (Cambridge, MA: Belknap Press of Harvard University Press, 2007).

B. Alan Wallace, ed., *Buddhism and Science: Breaking New Ground* (New York: Columbia University Press, 2003).

PHYSICS

We have looked at the different forms that the religion–science debate takes in the different world religions. Now, in this and the following two chapters, science will take the lead. In each of these chapters we will work with the core theories and assumptions of a specific set of scientific disciplines. We will then explore the speculative questions that arise, directly or indirectly, out of these sciences. In the process you will become familiar with the proposals that have been advanced by thinkers from the different religious traditions, as well as with the criticisms that their claims have engendered.

Readers must judge for themselves which religious responses they find credible and which ones are implausible. There is no blanket answer. One must decide on a case-by-case basis what are the merits of each particular religious interpretation of the scientific theories and results.

Some scientists are extremely interested in the speculative questions that arise out of their disciplines – sometimes more in the philosophical questions, and sometimes more in the religious issues. As people who know the science well, they find it natural to follow questions beyond the boundaries of their particular field of specialization. Other scientists have no interest in (or time for) such debates. Finally, some are openly hostile to these speculations; they consider it highly regrettable that anyone would start with physics or biology and end up with religious conclusions. These are bona fide disagreements; there is no 'official scientific position' about whether such discussions are good or bad.

In two kinds of cases, however, scientists will generally join forces. The first is when the science is misrepresented, or when discussants claim that something is 'scientifically proven' when in fact no such consensus exists. To do these discussions well, one must always be willing to be corrected by specialists – and ultimately by the world itself – about which theories correctly describe natural phenomena.

The second guideline turns on the distinction between 'going beyond science' and 'contradicting science.' It is one thing to explore religious claims that empirical studies cannot verify or falsify; philosophers, for example, do this all the time. It is another thing to hold beliefs that would make the scientific study of the natural world as we know it impossible. Those who adopt *that* position should not be surprised when they encounter concerted opposition from practicing scientists. Such opposition is not (necessarily) anti-religious. It is chiefly motivated by the goal of conducting good scientific research and continuing to make progress in the growth of scientific knowledge.

WHY THE RELIGIOUS INTEREST IN COSMOLOGY?

Cosmology is probably the oldest area of study that has raised deep questions about the nature of the universe; it remains a central area of concern in the contemporary debates around the world. Of course, for millennia the cosmology in question was not really a part of physical science. It is interesting to recall that, as recently as 230 years ago, the great German philosopher Immanuel Kant could argue in his *Critique of Pure Reason* that cosmology was not *and could not be* a physical science. Today, however, cosmology is a mathematically precise field within physics, drawing on astronomy, astrophysics, and fundamental physics. Still, humans continue to ask the same sorts of questions about the cosmos as a whole, and to speculate about the same sorts of answers, as have been associated with cosmological reflection since the beginning.

It was the same Kant who wrote that the two strongest sources for belief in God are 'the starry sky above and the moral law within.' In this he is in good company. The Hebrew Bible (venerated by Jews, Christians, and Muslims alike) draws the same connection:

The heavens are telling the glory of God;
and the firmament proclaims his handiwork.
Day to day pours forth speech,
and night to night declares knowledge.
There is no speech, nor are there words;
their voice is not heard;
yet their voice goes out through all the earth,
and their words to the end of the world.

(Psalm 19: 1–4)

The Christian New Testament likewise links the 'starry skies above' with the 'moral law within':

[W]hat can be known about God is plain to them, because God has shown it to them. Ever since the creation of the world his eternal power and divine nature, invisible though they are, have been understood and seen through the things he has made. So they are without excuse.

(Rom. 1: 19–20, NRSV)

Certainly the experience of staring at the immensity of the heavens is religiously ambiguous. In some ways the natural human response when looking at the stars is, 'We are but a speck,' or, as the classic rock song put it, 'We are but a moment's sunlight/Fading in the grass.' Even the psalmist concludes, 'When I look at your heavens, the work of your fingers, the moon and the stars that you have established; what are human beings that you are mindful of them, mortals that you care for them?' (Psalm 8: 3–4, NRSV). In his classic study, *The Sacred Canopy*, the sociologist of religion Peter Berger describes the feeling of *anomie* (meaninglessness or lawlessness) that threatens human beings as they contemplate their smallness in the face of the universe.[1]

The universe suggests not only an immensity of space but also an immensity of time. Carl Sagan quotes an ancient Hindu myth in his well-known book, *Cosmos*:

There is the deep and appealing notion that the universe is but a dream of the god who, after a hundred Brahma years, dissolves himself into a dreamless sleep. The universe dissolves with him – until, after another Brahma century, he stirs, recomposes himself and begins again to dream the cosmic dream. Meanwhile, elsewhere, there are an infinite number of universes, each with its own god dreaming the cosmic dream. These great ideas are tempered by another, perhaps greater. It is said that men may not be the dreams of gods, but rather that the gods are the dreams of men.[2]

Yet humans have also derived a deep sense of religious meaningfulness from the cosmos. Many link the immensity of the universe to the greatness of God, the source whose power, knowledge, and wisdom were great enough to create it.

But ask the animals, and they will teach you; the birds of the air, and they will tell you; ask the plants of the earth, and they will teach you; and the fish of the sea will declare to you. Who among all these does not know that the hand of the Lord has done this? In his hand is the life of every living thing and the breath of every human being.

(Job 12: 7–10, NRSV)

When the immensity of the universe is linked to the greatness of God, it sometimes gives rise to the human response of worship. This response comes in several forms: worship of a Creator who must have been great enough to create such a universe, or worship because such an immensely powerful being would exercise providential care and concern for individual members of this creation. As Jesus is reported to have said, 'Are not two sparrows sold for a penny? Yet not one of them will fall to the ground apart from your Father. And even the hairs of your head are all counted' (Matthew 10: 29–30, NRSV).

Links between the immensity of the cosmos and religion arise in more indirect ways as well. One is an argument for transcendence based on a sort of analogy. The universe is so much larger and greater than we are, and humans are so finite, so puny, in comparison. It is hardly an exaggeration to say that, in its size and duration, the universe vastly transcends these tiny creatures who are limited to a measly 'threescore and ten' years. To some, that transcendence in turn gives rise to the idea of a being or a level of reality that is as much greater than, and as much transcendent of, the universe as a whole as it is of us. This higher reality is differently described in the various religions: God, Allah, Brahman, the Buddha Mind. Each religion testifies in its own way to this primordial transcendence.

Another traditional argument is similar to the first. We know ourselves as contingent, since we might not have existed. But the universe, too, in all its immensity, is also contingent, since it does not include necessity within itself. It might have been different in certain respects or, indeed, it might not have existed at all. Therefore the universe as a whole must be grounded in a higher reality, a reality that exists necessarily. This reality is what the various religions refer to as the religious ultimate.

This 'argument from contingency' plays different roles in different religions. In the three Abrahamic faiths, for example (Judaism, Christianity, and Islam), it represents the religious ascent from a really existing, lawlike, but still contingent universe to a necessary and eternal Creator. An even more radical example is the doctrine of *maya* or illusion in traditional Hinduism. This core Hindu belief not only asserts that Brahman is immensely greater than the entire universe we perceive; it even claims that all that we perceive is, by contrast, merely illusion. The universe that scientists measure does not even exist because, ultimately, only Brahman does.

Of course, such language is a long way from the language (and mathematics) of physical cosmology today. We now know that this universe originated about 13.7 billion years ago from an initial state that physicists call a 'singularity.' The WMAP satellite has provided amazing images of the cosmic microwave background radiation, reflecting the state of the universe when it was less than 400,000 years old. By combining astronomical measurements with knowledge from particle physics, cosmologists can reconstruct the various stages of cosmic evolution with great precision.[3]

Many respond that *this* story, and not some set of ancient myths of the origin of the cosmos (cosmogenies), should be the object of belief for contemporary men and women. Is science not the more authoritative and reliable source? Indeed, should we not say that 'this is all that exists, and there is nothing else'? Bertrand Russell, for example, the great twentieth-century atheist philosopher, famously upheld this position in a BBC radio debate with Father

Frederick Copleston, which was aired live on January 28, 1948. Bertrand Russell argued that if one can explain every finite entity and occurrence in terms of natural laws and other finite phenomena, there is no need to postulate a higher or deeper level of reality. And, he added, science by its very nature *does* explain every particular object or event in terms of other finite objects, events, and laws. The role of God as the ground of all things is therefore rendered otiose.

Yet others have continued to find deep religious motivation in the existence of the cosmos. Clearly, religious accounts of the ultimate origin of the universe have continued to flourish in the era of scientific cosmology. This awe or wonder sometimes expresses itself as the sense of something deeper that underlies the appearances.[4] Sometimes it manifests in the explicit belief in a Creator God. And sometimes the beauty of the mathematics, the regularity of natural laws, and the power of the scientific explanations themselves seem sufficient grounds for wonder.

FUNDAMENTAL PHYSICS

If there is 'magic' in science, the greatest magic must lie in the most fundamental science: particle physics. Both among scientists and in the public at large, fundamental physics is often seen as holding the key to a scientific understanding of the entire natural world. Already Simon Laplace's parable of the 'demon' caught the popular imagination in the early eighteenth century:

> An intellect which at a certain moment would know all forces that set nature in motion, and all positions of all items of which nature is composed, if this intellect were also vast enough to submit these data to analysis, it would embrace in a single formula the movements of the greatest bodies of the universe and those of the tiniest atom; for such an intellect nothing would be uncertain and the future just like the past would be present before its eyes.[5]

The complete determinism of this particular picture did not survive the advent of twentieth-century quantum mechanics, but the fascination of the vision of a 'grand unified theory,' a 'theory of everything,' most certainly has. Part of the mystique lies in the incredible precision of fundamental physics. There are predictions in solid state physics that can be verified to eight significant digits. As Nobel Laureate Robert Laughlin points out, that would be like making a prediction of the population of the United States and not missing by a single person.[6]

Another part of the mystique of fundamental physics lies in its ability to detect earlier mistakes and to produce ever more precise predictions of measurements. The great advocate of falsifiability as the defining feature of science, Sir Karl Popper, liked to describe the expedition, led by Sir Arthur Eddington, which journeyed to the west coast of Africa in 1919 in order to test Einstein's general theory of relativity. Einstein's theory predicted that the light from distant stars should bend as it passes by the sun. Thus specific stars, whose location is well known to astronomers, should appear to be in a different location after their light has passed close to the sun. The 1919 eclipse thus provided the perfect opportunity to falsify Einstein's claim. As you probably know, Einstein's risky prediction succeeded, and – at least as Popper tells the story – this remarkable fact propelled Einstein's general theory of relativity to the center of scientific attention. (As often happens in the history and philosophy of science, the actual story in the history of science is rather more complex and less black and white.)

Other reasons for the fascination with fundamental physics include the level of consensus among scientists and, for outsiders, the sheer opacity of the complex equations that are the lifeblood of this science. Perhaps for these reasons, the fundamental laws of physics have been taken by religious persons to express the means by which God may have created the cosmos. Thus Galileo famously distinguished between the Book of Scripture and the Book of Nature. They are two separate 'books,' he said, one written in human words and the other in the language of mathematics, yet both express the nature of God and God's creative activity. Perhaps nobody has put the point more concisely than Alexander Pope in his famous couplet:

Nature and Nature's laws lay hid in night:
God said, 'Let Newton be!' and all was light.

For whatever reasons, the connections between fundamental physics and religion have often appeared to be some of the most significant and fascinating. By the same token, the tensions and apparent incompatibilities between fundamental physics and religion have seemed to many to be the most powerful of all.

Fine-tuning and the multiverse

In the science–religion debate, the precision of physics cuts both ways. Take the fundamental constants of nature, for example. These include constants such as the mass of the electron, the strength of the weak and strong nuclear forces, the ratio of protons to electrons, the expansion rate of the universe, the speed of light, and so forth. Given the exactness of our knowledge of these constants and the roles they play in nature, physicists in the twentieth century were able to show that life as we know it would have been impossible if the constants had even slightly different values.

All this led the physicist Bernard Carr to formulate an idea that he called the 'Anthropic Principle': it is as if the universe was designed or 'fine-tuned' for life, even intelligent life, since if the fundamental values had been even slightly different, no life at all could have arisen. John Barrow and Frank Tipler won broad interest for this topic with their highly influential 1986 book, *The Cosmic Anthropic Principle*.[7] Although Barrow and Tipler did not draw any strong theological conclusions in their classic work, many others who were influenced by their arguments did. If the fundamental laws and constants of nature are indeed precisely what they would have to be for intelligent life to emerge, then (some have argued) the best explanation is that *God* established these laws and constants in order to bring about intelligent life, or even with the intention of producing human beings in particular.

Note that the recent fine-tuning debate is in many ways distinct from the debate about Intelligent Design that we discussed in Chapter 2. In this case people weren't claiming that the theological conclusions that one might draw from the fine-tuning argument were themselves a part of science; they would be (at best) philosophical implications of the science. Nevertheless, the Anthropic Principle spawned passionate responses from both theists and atheists.

Critics emphasized the analogy with a lottery. If you win the lottery, you may be inclined to wonder who designed the lottery such that you would be the winner in the end. But of course it was not designed for *you* to win it. The outcome was random: someone had to be the winner, and it just turned out that your ticket was drawn. The initial odds against your winning may have been (say) 20,000,000 to 1. But of course, once your ticket had been drawn, it was suddenly irrelevant what the prior odds were. Once you have won – even if the outcome was random – it doesn't really matter how improbable it was in advance. So also with humanity: we have arisen out of a long process of cosmic evolution, but it doesn't follow that the universe was designed to produce *us*.

As it happened, 'multiverse theory' was born about the same time. Some of the physicists involved in formulating the dominant model of the origin of the universe, Inflationary Big Bang cosmology, began to argue that the mathematics suggests that other universes with different laws and constants should also exist.[8] To opponents of the Anthropic Principle, this was the nail in the coffin for theologies of fine-tuning. 'Not only is it wrong to infer a designer from the fact that we're here,' they argued,

> it looks like there are many – possibly indenumerably many – universes. In many of these it will be physically impossible for living beings to arise. No divine being created our particular universe with the intent to produce life. Instead, there are infinitely many universes, only a small proportion of which could contain living things. That our particular universe includes us requires no further explanation. Given the immense number of universes, it was statistically likely that at least one universe would happen to have the right physical conditions for the emergence of life. As long as there is nothing special about this particular universe, the fine-tuning argument fails.

This influential argument leaves theists with four basic responses. They can concede the point and withdraw the fine-tuning argument. Or they can argue that because the scientific evidence for such a multiverse is insufficient – after all, claims about causally separate universes could never be empirically tested – the multiverse theory itself should pass as philosophy or wishful thinking but not as a real scientific hypothesis.[9] Third, perhaps God chose to create the whole ensemble of universes in order that life could arise in *some* of those universes – a conclusion that is clearly consistent with the idea of God. Finally, theists could argue that some kind of fine-tuning applies even on the multiverse model. For example, if the multiverse theory is to be a scientific theory, there must be laws and constants that hold across *all* universes. In fact, these laws will be even more clearly independent of any given physical universe, since they govern the entire ensemble of universes. But that result suggests an even stronger theological conclusion, namely that God designed the underlying laws that would produce this incalculably infinite number of universes.

Many of the early defenders of the fine-tuning argument have since conceded that the use of the term 'anthropic' was mistaken. The better term, they now argue, is that this universe is *biophilic*, that is, friendly to the emergence of life. One would have to construct a separate argument, based in the biological sciences, that life, once it emerged, would inevitably give rise to human beings. (We return to this argument in the next chapter.) Put differently, at present it accords better with the physical evidence to affirm that this universe is a biophilic universe, that the laws and constants are fine-tuned to make it possible for life to arise and that, were they even slightly different, life could not have arisen. Whether or not a biophilic universe makes it likely that God exists continues to be a contentious question.

Quantum physics and consciousness

Many times the deepest connections between scientific theories and religious questions are mediated through philosophy. Although it is common to draw more direct links from science to religion – sometimes in ways that are congenial to the interests of religious persons, and sometimes in ways that are highly critical of them – what some people think of as direct entailments often turn out, upon closer examination, to be rather less obvious. By contrast, when one's underlying philosophical commitments are clearly stated and their roles in one's arguments are brought to light, much more rigorous accounts of the science–religion relationship can be constructed – and criticized. Quantum physics provides the best example of this pattern.

Quantum physics, or quantum mechanics, is the study of physical systems at scales smaller than the atom. Central to the study of these systems is the wave function, which describes the probability of measuring a particular subatomic particle at a particular place or with a particular momentum. Quantum physics is an extremely precise predictive science, often far more precise than the study of macrophysical systems. But it has also produced some amazing paradoxes, which in turn have given rise to some rather remarkable attempts to interpret and explain what physicists observe.

One of the most famous proposed solutions is the Copenhagen interpretation of quantum physics. This view, named after the city where physicists originally formulated the core concepts of quantum physics in the late 1920s, claims to answer some of the deepest problems raised by quantum mechanics. One of the centerpieces of quantum physics, the Schrödinger equation, describes the evolution of a quantum system as a continuous function. But when we measure a quantum system – say, a beam of light – at some specific place and time, we generally observe a discrete subatomic particle, such as a single photon.

This paradox, known as the 'measurement problem,' calls for an explanation: what causes the 'collapse' of the wave function into discrete, measurable states? The Copenhagen or 'orthodox' interpretation was that *it is the act of the observer, the measurement itself, that causes this collapse*. Thus, for example, if a beam of light is split into two beams and then allowed to strike a screen, one sees the interference effects that are typical of wave dynamics. But if one measures one of the beams on its way to the screen (the so-called two-slit experiment), the interference effects disappear, and the observer detects only the marks of discrete photons hitting the screen. The measurement, it is said, 'collapses' the wave into individual photons of light, so that no wave interference pattern is detected.

The Copenhagen interpretation was the most dominant interpretation of quantum mechanics for some 50 years, and many well-known physicists still speak in these terms today. However, from the beginning people recognized that the Copenhagen 'solution' itself begged for philosophical interpretation. What is it about the measurement by an observer that causes the collapse of the wave function? A number of interpreters claimed that it is *the consciousness of the observer* that is responsible. Thus in a famous thought experiment, Erwin Schrödinger imagined that a cat is locked inside a sealed case, cut off from interaction with the outside world. Inside the case a quantum mechanical trigger (say, radioactive decay) is linked to a capsule of cyanide. If the radioactive material decays, a mechanism is triggered, the cyanide gas is released, and Schrödinger's cat dies; if not, the cat lives. At the end of a week, the physicist opens the case, at which time she either finds a very dead cat or a very hungry cat.

Now, according to the standard interpretation the collapse of the wave function does not occur until the case is opened and the cat is observed. Until then there is only the quantum state described by the Schrödinger wave function. The mathematics suggests that during this time there is a 'superposition' of the two possible outcomes: 'dead cat' and 'live cat.' So, on this interpretation, the cat is actually existing in a quantum superposition ($|$dead cat$>$ + $|$live cat$>$) – that is, *simultaneously in both states* – until the moment of observation. The observation by the scientist then resolves the superposition, the both/and state, into one or the other outcome, and she finds either a dead cat or a live cat. On the standard interpretation, then, the world is indeterminate until the moment of measurement; only then does the world become one way or the other.

Why is it that the *cat's* awareness is not enough to resolve the superposition? The Copenhagen theorists assumed that consciousness was somehow necessary to bring about the collapse and that only humans are conscious. But will *any* consciousness suffice, or must it be the consciousness of a physicist who understands quantum mechanics? In a play on the Schrödinger's cat thought experiment – some view it as a *reductio ad absurdum* – Eugene Wigner imagined placing not a cat but his friend in the case for a week. Imagine that Wigner's friend knows nothing about quantum physics. Would we say that Wigner's friend *also* exists in a state of superposition ($|$dead friend + $|$live friend$>$), until the box is opened, at which time the physicist finds either a dead friend or a very hungry (and very angry) friend? Does the collapse require a physicist who understands the mysteries, or at least the mathematics, of quantum mechanics?

In any event, according to the Copenhagen interpretation an act of observation, hence consciousness, is required to resolve quantum potentialities (superpositions) into actual macro-physical states. This hypothesis gives rise to still further specula-tions. For example, could quantum physics, so understood, help to resolve the ancient paradox of brain and mind? The famous Berkeley physicist Henry Stapp, following suggestions from von Neumann,[10] has argued in just this way in recent years. Stapp relies on the Copenhagen interpretation of quantum mechanics to suggest how the mind could have effects in the physical world without breaking the laws of physics. He maintains that the brain is a natural system that has evolved over time to enable conscious observations. Each conscious observation resolves quantum inde-terminacies (superpositions) into specific macrophysical states, thus changing the world in some way. This would explain how humans can form free, conscious intentions that actually cause changes in the physical world, enabling us to carry out inten-tional actions. Similarly, at one point Roger Penrose and Stuart Hammerhof suggested that the tiny brain structures known as microtubules are small enough that quantum effects are relevant to computing their dynamics.[11] Microtubules, they argued, could be the (or a) mechanism by which the brain utilizes quantum effects to consciously influence the world.

Others went even further. The famous Princeton physicist John Wheeler argued that, according to the Copenhagen model, a photon of light could travel for (say) 300 million light years from a distant galaxy, the whole time remaining a quantum-potential-to-be-observed, until the moment that it struck the eye of a conscious observer (for example, you) as you stand observing the stars late at night. At that point it retroactively becomes an actual event – retroactively, that is, backwards in time over 300 million years and backwards in space over that immense distance.

Generalizing this suggestion, Wheeler pictured the universe as a capital U, starting at the Big Bang and moving down the U and back up the other side. He then placed an eye at the end (see Figure 4.1). On this hypothesis, the universe itself remained in a state of quantum potentiality until such time as the first conscious observers evolved. At whatever point conscious agents first observed the universe, the universe was *retroactively* brought into being, all the way back to, and including, the Big Bang.[12]

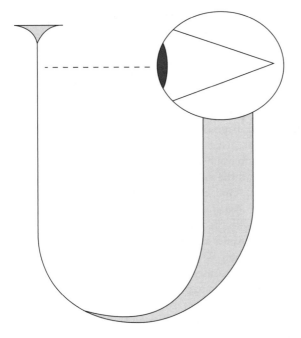

Figure 4.1 Collapsing the wave function of the universe: John Wheeler's proposal.

Possible religious implications

These thought experiments, and many more like them, are part of the standard lore of quantum physics, extending back some 80 years. One can agree or not agree with this or that suggestion without any religious motives or interest at all. But it only takes a moment's reflection to realize that these interpretations of the Copenhagen model are rife with potential religious implications.

If *our* consciousness is sufficient to transform a quantum state from potentiality to actuality, then wouldn't God's consciousness do the same? Is it more plausible to imagine that the first conscious human retroactively creates the cosmos, as John Wheeler did, or more plausible to postulate a God who was the original Observer? Advocates of this view hold that God's observation of quantum potentialities (which presumably God also created) could have been the means by which God brought the universe into being. Could it be that in every free intentional action we become 'co-creators' with God,[13] continuing to form the universe in accordance with, or perhaps in tension with, the original divine creative intent? Christian theologians have argued that this creative role is the essence of the 'image of God' (*imago Dei*), the concept they use to define the human person. This freedom to bring about states of affairs in the world, beginning with our own bodies and thoughts, they argue, is what makes us morally responsible; it is also what defines our responsibility before God.

Of course, not all the religious applications of quantum physics have been theistic. One of the earliest books in this genre was Fritjof Capra's *The Tao of Physics*.[14] Capra proclaimed that modern physics converges with the classic religious philosophies of the East. He suggested that physics in our time is now discovering the unity of all things in a single Way (Tao). The Tao is characterized by perfect harmony, the balance between oppositions (*yin* and *yang*). These oppositions are not oppositional; they are contrasts without contradiction. Von Weizsäcker famously claimed that in quantum physics wave and particle become complementary descriptions of the same basic reality.[15] This, Capra suggested, is what contemporary physics yields: the complementarity of particle and wave, of mind and matter, of energy and objects, of part and whole, of motion and rest, of mind and body.

Similarly, the Hindu physicist Amit Goswami interpreted the new physics as an opening to the ancient wisdom of the Vedas and Upanishads. He describes this new view of reality as *The Self-Aware Universe*.[16] One of the central Hindu teachings is of the unity of all subjects (Ātman) in a single, all-encompassing consciousness or awareness (Brahman). Quantum physics, he suggests, shows that each individual physical reality moves from potential to actual by means of a moment of awareness or consciousness on the part of Ātman. But the various Ātman are not separate; they are all components of a single self-aware source. The unification that physicists seek between the four fundamental forces would therefore represent the same salvation that the Indian sages have sought after: the unity of each individual consciousness (and each individual microphysical state) with the cosmos as a whole. The physical side of this unity would be described by a Grand Unified Theory

(GUT), which would include the reconciliation of quantum physics with general relativity; the spiritual side of the unity is expressed by the one enduring Brahman.

As a final example in this category, consider the work of the French physicist and agnostic Bernard d'Espagnat.[17] D'Espagnat begins with the framework of quantum field theory, arguably the most foundational physical theory at present. In this physics, what is primary is the quantum field; any individual particle is (according to the theory) a sort of distillation of the field at a particular time and place. We see the universe only through our equations, which describe it as a potential to be observed (a notion d'Espagnat derives from the early quantum physicist Niels Bohr). If all that we observe are potentials, then perhaps each one is an expression of an underlying, 'veiled' reality. That reality would transcend all the divisions that we experience: between observer and observed, between subject and object, between potential and actual, and so forth. But we can know nothing of the Real beyond our own perceptions and theories. D'Espagnat therefore makes a move reminiscent of Immanuel Kant: the notion of the Real is a 'limit concept' (*Grenzbegriff*); it points toward something that we can never actually know. Religion is an attempt to formulate this thing that cannot actually be known; thus it points beyond itself into mystery – though it may also be the mystery that sustains us.

Many more openings from science to religion arise here, as one speculates further about the nature of fundamental physics. One can see that in each case the theories, or at least the more interesting ones, are based on the best of our current physical knowledge. But each one then utilizes resources from the world's philosophical and religious traditions in order to conceive whatever ultimate reality may be hinted at in the equations and theories of our most fundamental physics.

WHAT PHYSICS DOES AND DOESN'T SHOW

If science and religion were intrinsically incompatible, then all mixtures of the two would be logically excluded. That is, a scientifically minded religious believer, or a scientist who takes a religious approach to his scientific work, would be contradictions in terms. In fact, however, not only are such blends *not* contradictory;

one encounters them with surprising frequency. Scientists frequently describe their work and the salvific role of science in religious terms. Indeed – and perhaps ironically – those who strive to wipe out religion in the name of science often do so by coloring science in explicitly religious terms, by utilizing unfalsifiable language, and by dividing the world into in-groups and out-groups using methods more often employed by religious groups.

Conversely, one increasingly encounters representatives of religious traditions (more often the more liberal or progressive wings of these traditions) who are ready to endorse empirical explanations of their canonical documents and religious experiences. They also describe their own belief in highly revisionist ways, conceding the ambiguous nature of the evidence and even of their own convictions. Many open-minded believers advocate blends of belief and doubt (or even skepticism) that are far more reminiscent of what we would generally call a scientific approach to hypotheses and uncertainty.

It is possible to argue, of course, that such persons are by definition *post*-religious, since they are not superstitious, dogmatic, or dismissive of other views, and they accept the possibility that they are wrong. But doesn't it beg the question to dismiss them for that reason? The more natural response is to conclude – as earlier chapters have also suggested – that religion is a rather more complex and nuanced phenomenon than some of its opponents (and advocates!) have suggested. At any rate, it at least appears to be possible to be scientific about one's religion and to be religious about one's science.

Indeed, this result suggests an interesting new hypothesis about the religion–science discussion as a whole. Is it possible that 'religion' and 'science' do not represent two utterly distinct sets of human attitudes and activities after all, but rather two different *tendencies* in human thought and action? On this view, one could be 'scientific' about any part of one's life: one's career, one's relationships, one's political attitudes, or one's own religious experiences and beliefs about ultimacy. Conversely, one could be 'religious' about one's profession, one's family, one's hobbies, one's data acquisition, one's theory formation – and even about one's science. In addition, one could also blend the two attitudes in a myriad of complex ways. In fact, it is probably better to use different terms to designate the end-points of the continuum. Perhaps it would be preferable to call them 'objective' and 'subjective,' or 'open-minded' and 'close-minded,' or thinking 'hypothetically' versus thinking 'dogmatically.'

Of course, even if one endorses this more nuanced way of looking at human thought and action, one might still conclude that those who hold religious beliefs and engage in religious practices still *tend* to be more 'close-minded,' whereas those who engage primarily in science and who eschew all religion *tend* to be more 'open-minded.' Note, however, that it is now an empirical question whether this correlation holds up; one would have to do some research to find out. One will also expect to find that the ways of being religious change significantly across cultures and over time, so that universal generalizations are difficult to draw. These complexities are part of the difficulty, but also the fascination, of the questions we are exploring. For those who are interested in the way the world really is, the complexities of the real myriad relations between science and religion are preferable to fixed preconceptions about what that relation *ought* to be.

QUESTIONS FOR REFLECTION AND DISCUSSION

1. Based on what you have read so far, how would you define the difference between 'scientific' and 'religious' modes of thought? Is one purely objective, reasonable, neutral, and hypothetical, while the other is inherently subjective, dogmatic, and unreasonable? Or are all of these categories present, to some extent, in both science and religion? Even if the differences are not black and white, are there *tendencies* for religion to be one way and science another? Try to define these tendencies, even if you cannot precisely define them.

2. In this chapter, we have looked at several attempts to integrate scientific and religious discourses. Do such attempts at integration add value to one or both discourses? Do attempts to blend the two produce new and interesting ideas, or are they dangerous for one or both sides? At this point in your studies, how would you evaluate claims for the (potential or actual) complementarity of science and religion?

3. Cosmology and fundamental physics can be sources of wonder for scientists and religious believers alike. How important is the physical world in your understanding of the religious or spiritual life? Does it point to God, or at least to a 'deeper dimension' of existence? Does science *require* a religious or spiritual interpretation? Is it *compatible* with such interpretations?

4. What are the limits of scientific and religious forms of thought? Can either side be carried out completely on its own, apart from any consideration of the other? Or is there some way in which the one gives rise to the other?

SUGGESTIONS FOR FURTHER READING

John D. Barrow, *New Theories of Everything: The Quest for Ultimate Explanation*, 2nd edn (Oxford: Oxford University Press, 2007).

John D. Barrow and Frank J. Tipler, *The Anthropic Cosmological Principle* (Oxford: Oxford University Press, 1986).

John D. Barrow, Paul C. W. Davies, and Charles L. Harper, Jr, eds, *Science and Ultimate Reality: Quantum Theory, Cosmology, and Complexity* (Cambridge: Cambridge University Press, 2004).

Peter Berger, *The Sacred Canopy: Elements of a Sociological Theory of Religion* (New York: Anchor Books, 1990).

Fritjof Capra, *The Tao of Physics: An Exploration of the Parallels between Modern Physics and Eastern Mysticism* (Boston, MA: Shambhala, 2000).

James T. Cushing, *Philosophical Concepts in Physics: The Historical Relation between Philosophy and Scientific Theories* (Cambridge: Cambridge University Press, 1998).

Bernard d'Espagnat, *On Physics and Philosophy* (Princeton, NJ: Princeton University Press, 2006), and *In Search of Reality* (New York: Springer-Verlag, 1993).

Amit Goswami, *The Self-Aware Universe: How Consciousness Creates the Material World* (New York: Putnam's Sons, 1993).

Stephen Hawking, *A Brief History of Time* (New York: Bantam Books, 1988).

Stephen Hawking and Leonard Mlodinow, *The Grand Design* (New York: Bantam Books, 2010).

Richard Laughlin, *A Different Universe: Reinventing Physics from the Bottom Down* (New York: Basic Books, 2005).

Henry P. Stapp, *Mind, Matter and Quantum Mechanics* (New York: Springer, 2009).

Alex Vilenkin, *Many Worlds in One: The Search for Other Universes* (New York: Hill and Wang, 2006).

Steven Weinberg, *The First Three Minutes* (New York: Basic Books, 1993).

Carl Friedrich von Weiszäcker, *The World View of Physics*, trans. Marjorie Grene (London: Routledge & Kegan Paul, 1952).

John Archibald Wheeler with Kenneth Ford, *Geons, Black Holes, and Quantum Foam: A Life in Physics* (New York: Norton, 1998).

THE BIOLOGICAL SCIENCES

Some of the most fascinating – and challenging – debates in the entire field of religion and science arise in biology. Perhaps it is no coincidence that the percentage of theists in biology is much lower than the percentage of theists in physics. The challenges to traditional religion stemming from biology are among the most serious in all of science. At the same time, developments in biology since Darwin, and in particular in the last decade or so, have provided significant impulses for fruitful development within religious thought. These two tendencies – an immense challenge to most traditional religious belief, combined with rich new resources for open-minded religious reflection – perhaps best convey the spirit of discussions about biology and religion today.

THE ORIGINS OF LIFE

> Then the Lord God formed man from the dust of the ground, and breathed into his nostrils the breath of life; and the man became a living being.
>
> (Genesis 2: 7, NRSV)

> So God created humankind in his image, in the image of God he created them; male and female he created them.
>
> (Genesis 1: 27)

From early in Western history the question of the origin of life, and especially of human life, provided one of the most significant places for identifying God's interaction with the world. Alongside the creation of the universe itself, surely this was the high point of God's intervention in the world. After all, how could what is living emerge on its own from lifeless matter? Are not the two types of existence fundamentally different? So one creation could not be enough; after creating the physical universe God would have to step in at least one more time – and perhaps many times, if He must separately create each species of living thing.

But there appeared to be an even more vital role for God to play: He had to create Man and Woman. After all, how could the distinctively human qualities – reason, mind or consciousness, and the sense of moral responsibility – emerge from 'mere matter in motion,' which is clearly devoid of such properties? How could it emerge from mere animals, the 'brutes'? Indeed, some theologians maintained (and still maintain) that God would have to intervene to create each individual human soul at the moment of conception.

These arguments, in one form or another, have provided perhaps the strongest impetus for affirming a literal reading of Genesis on the part of Christians, Muslims, and (in a few cases) Jews. The more moderate versions of this view hold that the 'days' of the first chapter of Genesis may not need to be literal, 24-hour days; they could reflect rough stages in the divinely guided evolution of the cosmos. But, most have maintained, surely at least three moments of divine creation are indispensable: the original creation of the cosmos, the first creation of a life form, and the separate creation of humanity. The first affirmation, that God is Creator, is axiomatic for theists; this term *defines* God. The second, that life is God's special creation, seemed just as clearly to be the only way in which one can do justice to the absolute qualitative break between the living and the non-living. The third, that God separately breathed a soul into the first human being, appeared necessary in order to preserve the uniqueness of human beings.

But science has not dealt gently with the second claim. (We return to the third in a subsequent section.) For it is equally axiomatic for scientists to seek to explain the natural mechanisms by which life has emerged. The research goes back to Stanley Miller and Harold Urey and their famous 1952 experiment.[1] They created a chemical mixture – commentators later called it the 'primal soup' – which was rich with the sorts of chemicals that scientists believe were present in the waters of the earth in the early stages of this planet. They then radiated the water with energy, as the sun would have done. Much to their amazement, Miller and Urey discovered that amino acids, the building blocks of life, began to form spontaneously.

Research on the origins of life has come an immense distance since this early experiment. Still, Miller and Urey's work remains significant as a way of illustrating how science works – in this field as well as in many others. We know a great deal about the chemistry of inorganic systems, as we do about the biochemistry of cells. The goal of science is to formulate and test hypotheses about how the transition from the first to the second could have occurred naturally on this planet. No divine intervention is, or can be, presupposed in providing these explanations. The scientific community experiences great excitement as, one by one the steps toward the complete explanation are achieved.

Experts in origins-of-life research have identified the precise tasks that have to be completed in order to explain how the first living, self-replicating organism could have arisen. About half of these tasks have already been completed, and scientists appear to be making good progress toward solving the remaining ones. Here's one account.[2] We already know how membranes form spontaneously in solutions in which chemicals called bilipids are present. We understand how a bilipid membrane, once formed, could contain within it biochemical processes, the antecedents to the metabolic functions that we observe in living cells today. We still need to understand how the presence of the right materials in the right density around the membrane could lead the membrane to open up at the right time, though the biochemistry of the process is not difficult to understand. Once it is open to the surrounding liquid, we understand how the instructions for building such a cell – call them proto-genes – could help it to make a copy of itself with the help of autocatalytic (self-catalyzing) processes. The new copy of the organism could then be surrounded again by a bilipid membrane. Once the various steps of this process have been put together and tested scientifically, origins-of-life researchers will have produced a full model of a simple biochemical structure – the precursor to the single-celled organisms that biologists study.

We already know well what happens once the first simple, self-replicating organisms have arisen. This was the central contribution that Charles Darwin (1809–1882) brought to biology: natural selection. Darwin did not know the structure of the DNA molecule or the way in which genes function, but he was able to work out in general terms the basic principles of biological evolution; later scientists then fleshed out the details. Once a self-replicating organism exists in an environment, a process of selection begins to operate. The specific informational content inside the membrane (call it cell A) will make more copies of itself if the right chemicals exist in its environment to catalyze this process. Imagine that, in the process, a mutation occurs, and a slightly different structure (call it cell B) forms. Imagine that cell B is able to make *many more* copies of itself from the chemicals in this same liquid medium. Biologists call this 'differential selection.' Cell B will continue to multiply until it becomes the dominant 'species' in this environment. Further mutations may then lead to other cell types that do even better in their common environment. Or imagine that cell types C and D use a slightly different set of chemicals to reproduce. When the A and B cells have used up all the chemicals on which they rely, C and D cells may begin to out-reproduce the others.

Further mutations lead to more and more complex organisms: ones with more effective outer membranes, perhaps, or ones that open up more quickly when the right chemicals are present, or ones whose processes are catalyzed by a broader range of chemicals. As the environment changes – and remember that organisms are important agents of change in their environments – mutations that were once neutral may now enable their cells to be more efficient at reproducing or at deriving nutrients from their surroundings.

Other mutations helped some cells to develop a simple chemical motor as a means of mobility. For example, cells with a tiny flagellum and with simple chemical sensors could move away from the toxic chemicals that would kill them and toward the nutrients that they need to survive and reproduce. Through further mutations, specialized structures gradually evolved, allowing for more and more complex behaviors and a more efficient use of resources. When the new, more complex structures caused their organisms to be better adapted to their environments, they outperformed the other organisms, made more copies of themselves (differential reproduction), and gradually assumed a more dominant place in their ecosystems. Selection, adaptation, and specialization continued as life forms spread around the planet. And the cycle continues into the present.[3]

EVOLUTION AND CREATION

All this will seem unobjectionable to scientists and students of science; but as soon as the question of God is raised, the situation changes. In fact, the debate over religion and evolution has become so explosive that some have quipped that God and Darwin mix about as well as oil and water.

Where to start? The pattern that we have noticed in earlier chapters emerges here as well. Two groups maintain the incompatibility of God and evolution, each one championing its particular cause and working to undercut the opposing group in every way possible. Since the media love a good debate, these two groups – let us call them *incompatibilists* – garner by far the greatest amount of public attention. A third, more irenic group, the *compatibilists*, then strives to show the compatibility of religion and evolution. Their writings are generally less well known, but they actually offer some of the most fascinating examples of work in the field. Let us trace the dynamics of this debate.

Atheist scientists such as Richard Dawkins take each advance in biology as further proof that religion is false.[4] The more we know about natural selection, they say, the more implausible becomes any notion of God as the Creator of life or as providentially involved in the world. Hearing this claim and this challenge, the other group of incompatibilists, conservative religious believers, increasingly tends to reject biology as a whole. A few years ago I listened to a woman summarize exactly this argument on National Public Radio: 'I know in my heart that God created me and takes care of the world, His creation. Biology today excludes any place for God. Thus I know that Darwin and his followers must be wrong.'

If you presuppose incompatibilism, then you can see her point. Assume for the moment that biology really has unlimited explanatory power. This means that it is able (without theological assistance) to account for the gradual development from non-living systems to living systems and on to more and more complex organisms, including the cultures and societies that they produce. Nothing remains to be explained. If this is true, then Richard Dawkins and his allies must be right; biology and God must be incompatible. "But," the religious opponent responds, "we know that God exists and is Creator. Since biology and creation are incompatible – that's the premise we share in common with Dawkins – it follows that biology *as a whole* must be wrong. Or, at best, it may identify a few of the mechanisms of how life works. But it *must* be wrong about the core principles of life, since they must be derived from God. With biology out of the way, we turn to the Bible for guidance on how the cosmos must have developed from the beginning until now."

A similar argument is used by the (many) Muslims who espouse 'Islamic Science' (see Chapter 3).[5] Individual bits of Western science may be helpful, they say: knowledge about the values of fundamental constants, or about the structure of water molecules, or about the anatomy of bears and their interactions with their environments. But, they say, we do know that the Holy Qur'an is incompatible with the assumption that evolution is random or 'unguided.' These Muslims then place the results of the specialized sciences within the Qur'anic religious and metaphysical framework, according to which God is fully in control of the progress of history from creation to the present. Islamic science will accept whatever results of the sciences fit with this core theological assumption, but it must discard the rest.[6]

A third option, rejected by both of these groups, seeks to preserve the most important features of both. Compatibilist positions such as 'theistic evolution' endorse scientific biology and welcome the increasing knowledge of the biosphere that it provides. They claim, however, that the important religious questions are left open by the scientific results. After all, questions concerning the ultimate origin or final purpose of the universe (if any) simply do not fall into the province of biology. One can accept the full biological account of evolution, and still believe, *at the religious or metaphysical level*, that a God underlies the evolutionary process and that evolution is somehow part of the divine creative intent.

So who wins? Each reader will either already have a favored position or can choose one as a hypothesis. The task is to identify the best reasons for and against one's own favored response, and then to see how the implications of one's own position fares in light of the data. The following two sections consider some important current debates within biology; they will provide further testing ground for your own hypothesis.

ARE GENES THE FUNDAMENTAL UNITS OF EVOLUTION?

Many people equate evolutionary theory as a whole with the *gene-centric perspective*. Darwin posited that there must be some carrier of heritable information, but a preliminary science of genetic information didn't really exist until Mendel performed his careful experiments on plants in the late nineteenth century. In the 1930s and 1940s the new genetic theory was fused with Darwinian biology in what came to be known as the New Synthesis or 'neo-Darwinism.' These genes, the units of biological information, code for proteins, which are the workhorses of the cell. When cells divide, genes provide the information that is necessary to construct a new cell. They thus contain the building plan for each organism; they are the blueprint, and organisms are the 'phenotypes' of their 'genotype.'

Perhaps the best-known manifesto of neo-Darwinism, at least among non-biologists, is Richard Dawkins' *The Selfish Gene*, which had sold over a million copies by the time the twenty-fifth-anniversary edition was published. 'Bodies,' Dawkins wrote, 'are survival machines that genes construct to make more copies of themselves.... We are ... robot vehicles blindly programmed to preserve the selfish molecules known as genes.'[7] Dawkins argued that both human selfishness and altruism can be explained by a more basic law which he called gene selfishness:

> I shall argue that the fundamental unit of selection, and there-fore of self-interest, is not the species, nor the group, nor even, strictly, the individual. It is the gene, the unit of heredity.... They are in you and me; they created us, body and mind; and their preservation is the ultimate rationale for our existence. They have come a long way, those replicators. Now they go by the name of genes, and we are their survival machines.[8]

Many have labeled this a reductionist position, since it apparently reduces evolutionary explanations to the genetic level. It is the genes that are selected for (or against) as the various phenotypes do better or worse in the struggle for survival. Of course, the 'machines' that the genes produce and the behaviors in which they engage can be extremely interesting. Genes have (on this view) evolved such interesting properties as booking vacations in Greece, inventing atom bombs, and advocating for world peace. Still, the purpose for which these machines and their behaviors exist is merely to serve the survival of the genes. (Of course, Dawkins is careful to emphasize that they don't *really* have purposes, though he speaks metaphorically as if they did.)

What about the more radical religious opponents to this view, those whose response is to reject evolution altogether? One cannot help but detect a certain irony here. In a manner strikingly similar to the gene-centric biologists, these religious opponents advance a position that evacuates most of the biosphere – and hence most organisms that have ever existed – of any real significance of their own. In order to emphasize the analogy, we might label this alternative to the *gene-centric perspective* the *God-centric perspective*. According to the anti-Darwinians, the real purpose of the biosphere was to produce human beings. Only human beings are *imago Dei*, made in the image of God; only they possess reason and rationality; only they are morally responsible. In its most extreme version, this view ascribes to the rest of creation only instrumental value: its value is only to serve as stepping stones, which lead to the ultimate appearance of what really matters: humanity.

It is interesting that René Descartes, the so-called father of modern philosophy, constructed a philosophy to which both parties appeal in order to promote their causes. For Descartes, animals and their bodies are 'mere machines.' They are devoid of souls, rationality, consciousness, and hence any value of their own. The God-centered perspective affirms that human beings have souls, whereas the gene-centric perspective denies this. But when it comes to the rest of the biological world, the two views turn out to be (somewhat surprisingly) significantly similar. For the gene-centric perspective, for example, all the real interest lies at the bottom of the ladder, at the genetic level. For the God-centric perspective, all the interest lies at the top of the ladder; it focuses almost exclusively on the emergence of *Homo sapiens* and on the God who brought about this species in order to be in relationship to Him. The rungs in between the top and bottom of the ladder – where the vast majority of organisms and their actions lie – are of only instrumental interest.

In recent years a third view has gained traction among biologists. Although it has not yet played much of a role in the evolution–and–religion discussion in the media, this new approach offers a richer account of how life works above the level of the gene and before the emergence of culture. Let us call it the *emergent systems perspective*, since it treats the biosphere as a series of systems within systems within systems. (Technically, this third view is a position in theoretical biology, or even the philosophy of biology, since it claims to identify a broader pattern that emerges out of the work of many individual biologists working in specific areas.)

Consider, as examples, three of the main contributors to the emergent systems perspective. Systems biology studies the system of all proteins or all metabolites within a single cell. Only by focusing on *patterns* of protein interactions, rather than on how individual proteins are derived from individual genes, can one recognize emergent properties in the protein system (the 'proteome') of a cell. Evolutionary developmental biology ('evo devo') recognizes emergent patterns of development in organisms – patterns that can be discerned only when one moves to the level of cellular interactions and when one includes the perspective of organismic development.[9] Finally, ecology studies interactions within ecosystems rather than particular organisms taken in isolation.

Biological systems are always embedded within larger systems, similar to the wooden Russian dolls that children open up only to find another smaller doll inside. From the emergent systems perspective, what might look like a simple organism, say, one that consists of only a single cell, in fact depends on a number of small subsystems. At the same time, an organism is not merely an aggregate of its subsystems; it carries out actions of its own and thereby becomes an actor in a broader system of actors. Organisms are thus more than the sum of their parts.

If this is right, the gene-centric perspective alone will not be able to tell the whole story of evolution; properties that emerge in the various systems above the level of the genome also make their own contributions to the explanatory story. But nor can approaches that are centered on human persons and their qualities suffice. Well before human beings came on to the stage, the biosphere was packed with living systems which contained many of the properties that we see manifested today in 'higher' organisms, albeit in more rudimentary forms.

A dramatic example of the emergent systems approach is found in a school known as *biosemiotics*.[10] For these thinkers, a unicellular organism is already a unit of meaning, interpretation, and purpose. In Darwinian terms, its purpose is to survive and reproduce, and actions that help bring about this purpose can be called purposive actions. This starting point, biosemioticians argue, is sufficient to provide all living organisms with a 'for-the-sake-of' structure. Stuart Kauffman puts it humorously: every organism is 'out to make a living' in its world.[11] Every organism is therefore an interpreting entity.

When a single-celled organism spins its flagellum in order to move up a glucose gradient and obtain more nourishment, it interprets the higher glucose concentration as a 'good' and acts in order to ingest more of it. Of course, the interpreting here proceeds solely at the chemical level (through osmosis and chemical bonding to the external cell membrane); no thoughts or mental attitudes or feelings are implied. Still, the three basic elements of interpretation ('semiosis') are already present: there is an interpreter; there is a state of affairs being interpreted; and there is an interpretation (in this case, the movement of the organism toward nourishment). There are also consequences: if the organism misinterprets a toxin as nourishment and moves toward it, it will die.

In a sense, it does not really matter whether you want to call these actions 'real interpretations' or merely 'proto-interpretations'; the broader point still remains. A continuum, a similarity-in-difference, runs from the simple 'interpretations' that unicellular organisms make when they respond to their environment, all the way through to the highly complex interpretations that human beings make when we (say) write a college paper on the meaning of Shakespeare's *Hamlet*. Step by step, the interpretations become more complex, more multifaceted, and more comprehensive as they embrace more dimensions of the environment.

According to the emerging systems perspective, *the program of biology is to reconstruct the ever-growing complexity of organisms, structures, and behaviors as one moves up the ladder of complexity from the simplest organisms to the most complex ones.* One will expect to find analogues of many human functions in more simple organisms. Simple organisms *perceive* their environment, though without eyes; they *know* things about what is around them, though without consciousness. They act to fulfill *goals*, though without conscious intentions. In short, they are biological *agents*. Sometimes biologists emphasize the continuities across multiple levels of the complexity ladder, and in other contexts they emphasize the discontinuities.

What does all this have to do with religion? Clearly biology in this sense does not provide irrefutable evidence of divine creation, in the way that Michael Behe's argument for 'irreducible complexity' was supposed to do (see Chapter 2). Nothing in the above account *requires* God or an 'intelligent designer.' At the level described, it is just what it appears to be: an account of evolutionary emergence in the way that many biologists understand it today. Yet the account also raises philosophical questions that one can formulate and debate. What is the significance of this gradual increase in complexity? What does it say about human persons, agents complex enough to know their own evolutionary history? Does it suggest that evolution is a directional process? Could evolution have a goal or meaning? Could it have been designed or directed in some way so that it would produce ever more complex agents? Which religious beliefs are compatible with such a possibility? Are any rendered (philosophically) more likely by this outcome?

ARE HUMANS UNIQUE?

Another major dispute concerns the continuities and discontinuities between *Homo sapiens* and other species, and hence the question of the uniqueness of human beings.

At first blush, the claim to uniqueness bumps into a fairly severe scientific challenge. After all, the categories of biology depend on similarities and differences among organisms. There are multiple ways in which organisms maintain their homeostasis or inner balance, many ways in which they move and perceive their environments, many ways in which they obtain nourishment, avoid predators and toxins, and reproduce. However, certain general principles obtain across all this diversity. First and foremost, organisms must adapt to their environment if the species is to avoid going extinct. They must reproduce and their offspring must themselves survive to reproductive age. They must take in nourishment and avoid predators.

Certainly, from the gene-centric perspective, the question of human uniqueness receives an unambiguous 'No!' We share some 96 percent of our genes in common with chimpanzees.[12] The laws of genetic variation and natural selection by the environment work the same way for snails, snakes, and human beings. By contrast, for the God-centric perspective, the answer is an unambiguous 'Yes!' Humans alone possess the theological properties we considered earlier. When one claims that humans alone possess souls and no other living beings have souls, one has made the discontinuity as sharp as it can be made.

The answer for the emergent systems perspective is rather more complex: 'Yes and no; it depends on what you want to emphasize.' No, humans are not unique in that (as we saw above) all of the qualities we possess are merely more complex versions of the simpler forms in which they occur in simple organisms. But yes: the *ways* in which we manifest these qualities are unique. Scientists such as Michael Tomasello[13] have studied the development of language and cognitive abilities in human and other primate infants, chronicling exactly at what points human performance diverges from anything we see in the other primates.

No one has expressed the differences more poetically than Melvin Konner. Konner, a naturalist, finds grounds for speaking of a major leap in the process of emergence, a step so significant that one is inclined to describe it as a qualitative break. He gives an example of the differences:

> In an engaging study of the conversations of three-year-olds, in the context of a longer chat between a boy and a girl, this occurred: 'Hello, Mr. Dinosaur.' 'Hello, Mr. Skeleton.' These three-word sentences probably contain enough complexity, enough levels of meaning, and enough imagination to ensure that comparable things will never be said by even the most brilliant talking ape.

I suspect that we are seeing the most rudimentary form of the key to being human: a sort of wonderment at the spectacle of the world, and its apprehensibility by the mind; a focusing, for the sheer purpose of elevation; an intelligent waking dream. In that capacity, perhaps, we find our greatest distinction, and it may be our salvation.[14]

Consider another example. Sue Savage-Rumbaugh has lived with a large group of bonobos in a house at the edge of a 16-acre forest for a number of years. Her work documents the advanced verbal abilities of these highly intelligent bonobos – indeed, forcefully enough that some scientists have challenged her for not retaining sufficient objectivity. Yet Savage-Rumbaugh is also very clear that humans have capacities for thought and language not matched by even the most intelligent bonobos.

Perhaps the best-known champion of our primate relatives is Jane Goodall. Her early work with chimpanzees in the Gombe Nature Preserve in Tanzania, Africa, set the stage for generations of fieldwork with primates, as well as providing powerful data about the unexpected cognitive and social capacities in non-human primates. I remember once hearing Jane describe a mother chimpanzee holding her dead child in her arms and mourning its loss over a period of several days – a phenomenon not observed in chimpanzees prior to this case. But at the end of the two-day period, Jane added, the mother set the dead baby down to go foraging and then simply failed to return to the baby when the group of chimpanzees moved on. After that, Jane saw no further signs of mourning or depression in the mother. Chimpanzees have physical, emotional, and mental experiences that are far closer to our own than many would expect, but this does not make their experience in the world identical to our own.

Why is the uniqueness question so important? Many – theists and atheists alike – have argued that human uniqueness is the key to human value. It is our uniqueness, some say, that justifies us in using animals in laboratory tests to determine, for example, whether medicines are safe or whether certain cosmetics might cause damage to our eyes. It is human uniqueness, others argue, that justifies us in being carnivores rather than vegetarians. From the God-centric perspective, the argument is easy: since animals don't have souls, they don't have an eternal nature, created to remain in communion with God. The earth and its non-human inhabitants exist for us to 'cultivate' and use. 'God said to them, "Be fruitful and multiply, and fill the earth and subdue it; and have dominion over the fish of the sea and over the birds of the air and over every living thing that moves upon the earth"' (Genesis 1: 28). In the language of the Qur'an, Allah placed us on earth to be 'vice-regents.' Hence it is our divinely ordained role to rule over all other life forms. Of course, it is better to be enlightened rulers rather than selfish despots; still, our place at the top of the ladder is assured. As we have seen, non-religious scientists can also appeal to structural and behavioral differences to make a similar case.

The emergent systems perspective approaches this question in a rather different way. It mitigates against making objective, black-and-white distinctions between humans and other animals. Some will say that our *greater degree* of mental ability, insight, and self-knowledge justifies us in treating other animals differently from how we treat human beings. Others will argue that the *continuities* between the species should make us more reticent about such actions. If animals suffer in ways sufficiently similar to how we suffer, then it is our obligation to prevent or minimize their suffering whenever possible, just as it is our obligation to prevent or minimize human suffering.

It is interesting to see what happens when the emergent systems perspective is placed in a religious context. It is perhaps easiest to trace in the Eastern traditions. Buddhists apply this mindset when they engage in compassion meditation. To practice compassion for all living things places them all into one category. Mirroring this spiritual practice, Buddhist metaphysics takes as its central tenet *pratītyasamutpāda*, or the principle of 'Dependent Arising' ('this being given, that arises'). All things arise out of all else; they are neither separate atoms nor the product of a single creator God. If all living things depend on each other and co-constitute each other, then it is wrong to make oneself an exception, treating other beings merely as means to one's own ends. Recent work on 'Engaged Buddhism' has turned this same core belief into a principle of activism.[15]

The Hindu traditions support a similar conclusion. All living things have Ātman (self or soul), and all Ātman are parts of the one Brahman, the one universal mind or consciousness that is the source of all things. This metaphysic, derived from the Vedas and Upanishads, provides strong grounds for treating all living things in a similar manner. Thus Hindus have been called from the beginning to be vegetarians and to care for other animals. Cows in the streets of Lucknow in Andre Pradesh, India's most crowded state, are treated with at least as much respect as human beings. You can watch traffic on a packed, eight-lane thoroughfare come to a screeching halt while one cow slowly saunters across the street.

The Jains hold some of the most radical standards in this regard, based (again) on the belief that *all* living things have a soul or *jiva*. A traditional Jain would walk down the path with a tree branch, sweeping the ground in front of his feet, lest he accidentally step on a bug or other small creature. The doctrine of reincarnation supports these ethical requirements. Suppose that there really is a gradual ascension of these souls or Ātman into more complex and more enlightened individuals, leading finally to the release from the cycle of birth and rebirth (*samsara*). In that case, there is indeed no ultimate difference between the self of the animal that you observe on the side of the road and you as the human observer. The animal deserves equal respect and care.

Indigenous religions emphasize the continuity across all living things perhaps even more strongly. 'Indigenous ways of knowing are not simply expressions of an instrumental rationality, or a functional, specialized knowledge framed exclusively for accomplishing specific tasks,' writes John Grim, a specialist in Native American religions. 'Native science is born of a lived and storied participation with the natural landscape.... Indigenous knowledge ... cultivates a deep empathy in relation to biodiversity, in which humans, within their own communities, often stand for voices in nature.'[16] He continues:

> The close connections between territory and society, religion and politics, cultural and economic life, are the intellectual and emotional basis whereby indigenous peoples maintain and recu- perate their knowledge systems.... This felt experience of indi- genous knowledge is that of beings-in-the-world who are mutually related and dependent on one another for survival, for

the knowledge needed to survive, and for the assertion of power that enables survival.[17]

Most of these views we have examined endorse some sort of human uniqueness. Even Richard Dawkins' *The Selfish Gene* seems to accept it: 'We are built as gene machines and cultured as meme machines, but we have the power to turn against our creators. We, alone on earth, can rebel against the tyranny of the selfish replicators.'[18] (The sentence is somewhat surprising, since the overall account in *The Selfish Gene* reads much more like a case for genetic determinism. If genes really are the survival agents and we are merely their 'machines,' one would have expected that any sense we might have of being able to guide our own fate would have to be interpreted as illusion.)

At the same time, except for the God-centered perspective all of these views accept the major continuities between humans and other animals. Putting the two conclusions together requires some sort of both/and position, one that leaves space both for similarities and for the differences. If this is correct, it provides an important framework for further discussion of evolution and creation. Religious answers that wish to be adequate to the biological evidence will have to mirror this structure of similarity-in-difference when they talk about the nature of human beings. A number of religious traditions are in the position to do this. Others, however, have some work to do in order to develop an anthropology (a theory of human nature) that does justice to the biological conclusions.

QUESTIONS FOR REFLECTION AND DISCUSSION

1. In what ways, if any, should contemporary evolutionary theory affect traditional religious understandings of nature? Could biology ever explain so much about the world that there would no longer be any room for religion? Or will there always be some openings for religious responses to nature, no matter how far the biological sciences advance?

2. Is the belief that there is an inherent value to nature or to living things a religious belief? Why or why not? How would you explain or justify such a belief?

3. Some people believe that Christians and Muslims, and perhaps other religious people as well, have to reject all biology since Darwin. Why do they think this? Do you agree with them? Or do you think there may be ways to harmonize biological conclusions and traditional religious belief? What might they be?

4. We considered the argument that there are interpreting agents at very early stages of biological evolution (biosemiotics). If this is true, how would it affect your understanding of human beings – or, for that matter, of the natural world around you? For example, would it have any ethical implications for how humans treat other species?

5. Melvin Konner suggests that the uniqueness of humans lies in 'a sort of wonderment at the spectacle of the world, and its apprehensibility by the mind; a focusing, for the sheer purpose of elevation; an intelligent waking dream.' What is he really claiming? Do you agree with him? Is humanity unique? If so, what makes us unique? If not, how does this illusion arise? Be ready to show how your religious or non-religious view of the world influences your answers.

SUGGESTIONS FOR FURTHER READING

Sean B. Carroll, *Endless Forms Most Beautiful: The New Science of Evo Devo and the Making of the Animal Kingdom* (New York: Norton, 2005).

Philip Clayton, *In Quest of Freedom: The Emergence of Spirit in the Natural World* (Göttingen: Vandenhoeck and Ruprecht, 2009).

Richard Dawkins, *The Selfish Gene* (Oxford: Oxford University Press, 1976).

David Deamer and Gail R. Fleischaker, eds, *Origins of Life: The Central Concepts* (Boston, MA: Jones and Bartlett Publishers, 1994).

Scott F. Gilbert and David Epel, *Ecological Developmental Biology: Integrating Epigenetics, Medicine, and Evolution* (Sunderland, MA: Sinauer, 2009).

Jesper Hoffmeyer, *Legacy for Living Systems* (New York: Springer, 2010).

Jesper Hoffmeyer, *Biosemiotics: An Examination into the Signs of Life and the Life of Signs* (Scranton, PA: University of Scranton Press, 2008).

Stuart Kauffman, *Investigations* (Oxford: Oxford University Press, 2000).

Sallie B. King, *Being Benevolence: The Social Ethics of Engaged Buddhism* (Honolulu: University of Hawaii Press, 2005).

Melvin J. Konner, *The Tangled Wing: Biological Constraints on the Human Spirit*, 2nd edn (New York: Times Books/Henry Holt, 2002).

Alessandro Minelli, *Forms of Becoming: The Evolutionary Biology of Development* (Princeton, NJ: Princeton University Press, 2009).

Massimo Pigliucci and Gerd B. Müller, eds, *Evolution: The Extended Synthesis* (Cambridge, MA: MIT Press, 2010).

Bharati Puri, *Engaged Buddhism: The Dalai Lama's Worldview* (New Delhi: Oxford University Press, 2006).

Sulak Sivaraksa, *Conflict, Culture, Change: Engaged Buddhism in a Globalizing World* (Boston, MA: Wisdom Publications, 2005).

Michael Tomasello, *Origins of Human Communication* (Cambridge, MA: MIT Press, 2008).

J. Scott Turner, *The Tinkerer's Accomplice: How Design Emerges from Life Itself* (Cambridge, MA: Harvard University Press, 2007).

THE NEUROSCIENCES

BRAINS, MINDS, AND CONSCIOUSNESS

No area of the debate between biology and religion has been more contentious than the debate about brains and minds. Without a doubt this topic hits particularly close to home, since it concerns the essence of who we are. What do the contemporary neurosciences – neurophysiology, neuroimmunology, neurochemistry, neuropharmacology, cognitive science – have to tell us about the nature of thought? Do they support or undercut the belief in the existence of souls?

Probably the hardest position to defend would be the view that what occurs in the brain has nothing to do with our thought. After all, if I have a stroke or a brain hemorrhage while writing this paragraph it will be less coherent than if my brain is functioning normally, and the text might make no sense at all. If you ingest drugs or a large amount of alcohol before reading this chapter or attending a lecture you are likely to experience it and recall it differently. (Probably it will strike you as funnier.)

Let us leave such strongly 'separationist' or 'dualist' positions aside for a moment, then, since there seems to be much evidence against them. (Don't worry; we'll return to them below.) This opens up space for the opposite response:

> Correlations between brain states and mental experiences are no big deal. After all, why should we care? All that matters is that scientists acknowledge that we have real thoughts and mental experiences, that our consciousness is not merely an illusion.

Perhaps, after a little more reflection, you add, 'Well, yes, and thought has to serve some causal function; it has to *do something*. As long as the neurosciences still allow us to say that our thoughts give rise to other thoughts and actions, we're okay. I intend to raise my hand, and a moment later my arm goes up. Isn't it obvious that my intention is the reason or explanation for why my hand was raised?'

But, it turns out, this is exactly what is in dispute in the recent debate. Francis Crick has formulated the implications of contemporary neuroscience in the strongest terms:

> The Astonishing Hypothesis is that 'You', your joys and your sorrows, your memories and your ambitions, your sense of personal identity and free will, are in fact no more than the behavior of a vast assembly of nerve cells and their associated molecules. As Lewis Carroll's Alice might have phrased it: 'You're nothing but a pack of neurons.' This hypothesis is so alien to the ideas of most people today that it can truly be called astonishing.[1]

On this view, consciousness is merely a by-product, and a causally ineffective one at that. What does the explanatory work, in everything we refer to as mental, is the architecture of neural connections and the electrochemically controlled bursts that race through it. Consciousness, contrary to public opinion, is merely a sort of superstructure. The 'how it feels' and 'what I intend' part only arises at the end of the day, as it were, *after* all the causal work has been done at the level of synapses, circuits, and neurotransmitters. As one neuroscientist told me at a conference a few years ago, 'Wires and chemicals, that's all we are – wires and chemicals.'

CAN THOUGHTS AND INTENTIONS *DO* ANYTHING?

This position is known as *eliminativism*.[2] The argument is simple: either neuroscience explains what happens in the brain or it doesn't. If it fully explains brain functioning, then there is really no place left for mental explanations. It couldn't be that *both* the mental and the physical explanations are true, because in that case neural events would be 'overdetermined' – that is, determined both by our thoughts *and* by the brain processes that our brain scans detect.[3] But that doesn't make sense: either science explains brain functioning or it doesn't. In short: once we have explained brain processes in neurological terms, it appears, there is simply no longer a place for mental things like thoughts and wishes to *do* anything in or to the brain.

What is the mental life, then? Do our experiences deceive us? The philosopher Daniel Dennett puts the result as follows: 'having an inner life – being something it is like something to be – is on this account a matter of having a certain sort of functional organization.'[4] He explains this position in a famous passage:

> Suppose an entity were all wired up in some fashion so as to realize the flow chart [of human cognitive functioning].... What would it be like (if anything) to be such an entity? At first glance the answer seems to be: not like anything. The whole system has been designed to operate in the dark, as it were, with the various components accomplishing their tasks unperceived and unperceiving. In particular, we have not supposed any inner introspecting eye to be watching ... And yet to us on the outside, watching such an entity, engaging it in conversation, listening to its efforts to describe the effects on it of various perceptual environments, there will be at least the illusion that it is like something to be the entity. In fact it will tell us (or at least seem to be telling us) just what it is like. But inside it is all darkness, a hoax. Or so it seems. Inside your skull it is also all darkness, and whatever processes occur in your gray matter occur unperceived and unperceiving. Can it be said that just as there is some other point of view that *you* have, there is some other point of view that *it* has?[5]

In the same way, Dennett suggests, the search for 'the self,' for the subjective center of the person, is nothing more than a category mistake:

> You enter the brain through the eye, march up the optic nerve, round and round the cortex, looking behind every neuron, and then, before you know it, you emerge into daylight on the spike of a motor nerve impulse, scratching your head and wondering where the self is.[6]

A correct understanding of the data, he suggests, deflates traditional notions of the self like letting air out of a balloon.

Of course, there are other possible interpretations than Dennett's. For example, mental experiences and feelings (*qualia*) could well exist as long as they don't *do* anything. If a quality arises out of a system but does not in turn influence that system, we call it an *epiphenomenal* quality. Hence *epiphenomenalism* is the view that humans (and perhaps other animals) do have mental and other experiences but brain states fully explain these mental experiences, since mentality arises out of the brain but does not in turn influence the brain in any way.

It would be fair to say that both of these strongly 'physicalist' interpretations of consciousness, eliminativism and epiphenomenalism, raise some difficulties for many of the world's religious traditions. Clearly these views are incompatible with traditions which argue that humans possess a non-material soul, spirit, or *Ātman*. At least at first blush, it appears that finding common ground between such beliefs and contemporary neuroscience is impossible. The spirit or soul that these religious traditions describe would be, by the very nature of the case, inaccessible to any scientific research. If the soul is supposed to have any effects on the functioning of the brain or body, one would expect those effects to be detectable, but most neuroscientists would say that no such effects are visible.

Or is it so obvious? One can in fact find articles and books in which believers attempt to give empirical proof of the workings of the soul or at least to specify how such effects could be detected. A colleague once proposed that one could scientifically verify the 'near-death' or 'out-of-body' experiences that are sometimes reported by people after they have been very close to death. These are the experiences where people report floating above their body and looking down on the doctors as they frantically try to save the patient's life. (In other cases, the patient later reports moving down a long, dark tunnel toward a light at the end, meeting an angel or other messenger of God, and being given the decision whether or not to return to the body.) My colleague suggested that researchers could attach three colored circles on the underside of each bed in the emergency rooms of a hospital. Under normal circumstances a patient would not see the colored circles; but if she had an out-of-body experience, she should be able to see things otherwise inaccessible to ordinary vision. Thus, he proposed, as soon as the person came back to consciousness after nearly dying, the researcher could ask her to name the three colors under her bed. If she could name them, this would prove that the soul can function separately from the body. (I leave it to the reader to judge the merits, and the morality, of this proposal.)

On a more serious note, many have cited the experiments of Benjamin Libet as indicating a causal role for conscious decision making. In these classic experiments, patients were asked to carry out 'freely voluntary acts' at a certain time, such as deciding either to lift or not lift their forefinger. The electroencephalogram (EEG) showed that these actions were preceded by 'a specific electrical charge in the brain,' which occurred about 550 milliseconds before the action and which Libet called the 'Readiness Potential.'[7] The readiness potential, he argued, was the impulse that, unless obstructed, would eventually produce the physical action of raising the finger. But then, at about 350 msec before the action, it became conscious (say, as the thought, 'I'm about to raise my finger'). At this point the person could choose to stop herself from acting. Libet commented, 'But the conscious function could still control the outcome; it can veto the act. Free will is therefore not excluded.'[8]

Libet claimed that his results were evidence that human beings have the ability to consciously veto actions that have already been set in motion by their brains. This veto ability is sufficient to show that we can consciously influence our body's actions, which means that 'we' are not identical to our bodies. It is also sufficient, he said, for us to count as free agents. Many advocates of human agency have taken the Libet results as evidence that consciousness plays a causal role in human actions – even if all that it can do is to veto actions already set in motion at an unconscious level by the brain. Jews, Christians, and Muslims have used the results to defend their claim that humans can be responsible before God for their actions. We are responsible for our virtuous actions, and for our sins; and God can rightly reward or punish us for them. Not surprisingly, these arguments have raised considerable controversy among scientists and philosophers, and various studies have been published to attempt to refute Libet's data or the uses to which he and others have put them.

Of course, advocates of the soul can pursue a different strategy altogether. They can argue that, since the soul is an immaterial substance, its effects simply cannot be detected by empirical means such as brain scans.[9] Souls operate according to some form of spiritual energy, so they don't consume any specific amount of natural energy in the world. This view is consistent, for example, with the traditional Catholic view that the soul is imparted to the fertilized egg at the moment of conception.[10] Likewise, some Hindus have argued that the entire empirical world that seems to surround us is in fact *maya*, that is, pure illusion. Thus, they respond, we do not need to be concerned if no evidence for the reincarnation of the soul can be found in this world. In fact, the Hindu may argue, it is the soul across its many lives that is actually real, whereas the sciences that pretend to verify or falsify belief in the soul are actually based wholly on illusion.

Admittedly, this strategy has also come under fire. 'If the soul is invisible,' critics complain, 'and its presence can never be detected, what reason do we have for affirming that a soul is present and active? Why not give up this postulation altogether?' Critics sometimes draw parallels with John Wisdom's famous critique of divine action. In his parable of the garden, Wisdom described a gardener in whom some people believe, a gardener who was said to be invisible and his actions undetectable. The believer and the nonbeliever debate whether the gardener really exists. 'At last the Sceptic despairs,' writes Wisdom. '"But what remains of your original assertion? Just how does what you call an invisible, intangible, eternally elusive gardener differ from an imaginary gardener or even from no gardener at all?"'[11]

WHATEVER HAPPENED TO THE SOUL?

Some religious persons have found this entire pursuit of the soul and its actions unproductive. They believe that talk of souls will come into increasing conflict with science – and the conflict is unnecessary. Thus in *Whatever Happened to the Soul?*[12] a group of Christian scholars now argue that Christians should never have signed on to the soul idea in the first place. This rejection of immaterial souls by a prominent group of Christian authors opens up an altogether different kind of discussion between religion and science – one that stands much closer to the 'emergent systems perspective' that we discussed in the previous chapter.

The religious argument goes something like this: 'We do not need to postulate the existence of an invisible, immaterial soul. But we do need to defend the reality of conscious action, free will, moral responsibility, and spiritual experience. Why not view such qualities as emergent *properties* of human beings, arising from their complicated brains and social interactions? Of course, what *has* these properties is the physical organism, the individual human being. But what emerges *out of* those neural firings is that set of properties that we call the human person. Emergent complexity in the natural world produces some amazing qualities. Gradually an animal evolved that is concerned with value, responsibility, truth, and even with her (real or imagined) relationship to the Ultimate. No natural laws are broken when one affirms that such qualities emerge naturally, and no occult entities such as souls or spirits need to be affirmed. Human persons, and the webs of value and meaning that they inhabit, are more than just a set of neural firings; they are emergent phenomena within the natural world.'

This is a fascinating compromise, since it appears to be thoroughly scientific and yet still allows for the emergence of persons as we know them. A number of scientists have been drawn to emergence theory as a result.[13] However, emergent complexity is not without its controversies. 'Not so quick,' the naturalistic opponent of religion may respond.

> As an epiphenomenalist, I am willing to admit the existence of subjective experiences (unlike my eliminativist colleagues, who deny their very reality). But you haven't yet gotten around the problem. The question is whether such properties really *do* anything, for example, whether they influence the brain. On the one hand, if you claim that they do, then you are no better off than the dualist with his idea of a soul. On the other hand, if the qualities that you imagine don't in fact have any causal influence in the world, then you are in effect affirming the very position that I affirm. In either case, how have you helped to reconcile science and religion?

This is indeed a serious worry: what good are traditional religious qualities if they don't in fact *do* anything in the person or her actions? The defender of the 'emergentist' interpretation of religion can make one of three responses. First, she can say that the only thing that matters is that people have experiences they can label 'religious' or 'spiritual.' If religious people experience spirituality or the presence of God, or if they feel sin or moral responsibility before God and persons, that's enough – whether or not these experiences really act as direct causes in their bodies. There is brain activity in the lower temporal lobe and the person experiences a sense of timelessness and peace; this is all that matters.

Second, the 'emergentist' religious person may argue that the naturalist objector is just looking in the wrong places. When you examine an fMRI or EEG, you shouldn't expect to find things like commandments or morals or spirituality directly increasing brain blood flow or causing neurons to fire – that's absurd. The appropriate place to look for religious properties is at the level of interacting persons, or at the level of cultural beliefs and practices. In the social sphere, for example, humans are quite skilled in recognizing when a person has acted morally or immorally toward other human beings or animals. The critic begs the question by pretending that, if one doesn't explicitly recognize moral obligations or spiritual experiences in the brain, they don't exist and influence what we do.

Third, religious people can try to provide arguments that mental states and properties in fact *do* affect what bodies do. You intend to finish your course reading before meeting up with friends, and what your body does corresponds with that intention. Why should we *not* say that your intention caused your actions? A person builds up moral character through religious practices and intentions extending over many years, and all who know her agree that she is a person with a deep spirituality and religious commitment. Why should we deny that her intentions had something to do with this outcome?

There is other evidence that one's mental attitude matters. For example, medical studies show that people who are depressed have less effective immune systems and slower recoveries, whereas people who are hopeful and optimistic tend to recover more quickly. Studies of the 'placebo effect' reveal the incredible power of mental expectations on how the body responds. In some of these studies, believing that the pills one is taking contain an effective medicine does just as much to speed recovery as actually receiving regular doses of the medicine itself! What better evidence could we have that intentions matter? It may well be that neuroscience and brain scan techniques do not yet allow us to detect the appropriate causal interactions so that we can explain them scientifically, but that does not mean that they don't exist.

STRICT NATURALISM, BROAD NATURALISM, AND PUSHING THE BOUNDARIES

These are fascinating and subtle debates, made possible by amazing developments in neuroscientific theory and scanning techniques over the past few decades. What conclusions should we draw from the previous three sections?

For those who pay close attention to the scientific data, it has become increasingly difficult to view the human person as a *purely* spiritual entity. One may wish to say that what really does the thinking and feeling within us is an immaterial soul, one that rises above physical causes. But such strongly 'dualist' claims become harder to sustain as we come to understand more and more of the neurological causes of our psychological states and as researchers develop 'designer medications,' namely drugs that have very precise and predictable effects on people's inner experiences (see Chapter 8). Of course, souls may still exist; but if they do, their effects are far harder to ascertain in the age of neuroscience than previous generations of philosophers ever realized.

What then of 'naturalistic' understandings of the human person? The *Encyclopedia of Philosophy* defines naturalism as the view that 'nature is all there is, and all basic truths are truths of nature.' It turns out, though, that the contemporary discussion is taking place between sharply different types of naturalists. On the topic of mind or consciousness we can divide them, I suggest, into two main camps: 'strict' naturalists and 'broad' naturalists.

Strict naturalists emphasize that the incredible predictive and thera-peutic power of the neurosciences overturns traditional commonsense views about what we are – and thus about our allegedly religious or spiritual nature. In the mid-twentieth century, the British philosopher Gilbert Ryle challenged what he called 'the myth of the ghost in the machine,' and his challenge has continued to have a major influence on many of the most famous Anglo–American philosophers over the past 60 years. According to the strict naturalist, it is high time to adjust our views of ourselves to the scientific data and the scientific world-view. Thus in a newspaper article the neurophilosopher Baroness Susan Greenfield spoke of her successes in dispelling the illusion of an 'I' that lies at the center of her thought and action. Another strict naturalist, Daniel Dennett, coined the term 'Cartesian theater' to ridicule the idea of a central 'I' or consciousness:

> Cartesian materialism is the view that there is a crucial finish line or boundary somewhere in the brain, marking a place where the order of arrival equals the order of 'presentation' in experience ... [Yet] the persuasive imagery of the Cartesian Theater keeps coming back to haunt us – laypeople and scientists alike – even after its ghostly dualism has been denounced and exorcized.[14]

Viewing ourselves as free, responsible, intentional agents is nothing but that: a view that we take of ourselves, which Dennett calls 'the intentional stance.'[15] We may be, as Francis Crick claimed, 'nothing but a pack of neurons,' but we are (somehow) able to view ourselves as intentional agents. Exactly how remains unexplained. David Chalmers calls this the 'hard problem' for the philosophy of mind: how can 'third-person' descriptions of neural functioning ever capture 'first-person' mental experiences (*qualia*)?

Many will find the agenda of the strict naturalist unnecessarily constraining and insufficiently justified. Are not two things true: that neurological interactions explain much of what we do, and that they do not explain *all* of what we do? The second group of naturalists, like the first, wants to pay close attention to scientific data and to take scientific explanation as far as it will go. But this group also thinks that human existence includes dimensions that go well beyond what scientific laws can describe. Elsewhere I have called these thinkers the 'broad naturalists.'[16] Because they are naturalists about the human person, broad naturalists do not affirm the existence of a soul or miracles; but they do believe that 'the person as a whole' has (and is affected by) properties other than strictly neurological processes.

Sometimes they use the analogy with a computer. Electronics and the laws of physics explain what the processor is doing; if it weren't for these laws, the computer wouldn't function. But *why* the processor is carrying out these particular steps can be explained only when one includes the intentions of the programmer and the person typing on the computer. Two things can be true at the same time: the computer user intends to send an email or solve a differential equation, *and* the microprocessor is functioning in ways that physics can explain. Similarly, neuroscientists can explain the operations of the brain, the 'hardware' of the human person. But what she is thinking, feeling, or intending as a person requires a different level of analysis. In fact, we have a set of empirical sciences that gather data and construct theories about these other aspects of human existence, namely the social sciences (psychology, sociology, and cultural anthropology). These social sciences do not need to be reducible to neuroscience, genetics, or physics in order to be bona fide sciences. They of course still presuppose that no laws of physics or biology are broken when a person decides whether to confide in another person or to distrust her. But distinctly human actions require *human-level* explanations.

This leads us to one final question: is even broad naturalism enough? Or should one push against the boundaries of naturalism as a whole? Moreover, can one be a naturalist and still be a Christian, Jew, Muslim, Buddhist, or Hindu?

RELIGIOUS EXPERIENCE

About ten years ago *Newsweek* ran a story on 'the God Spot.'[17] The research of the San Diego neuroscientist V. S. Ramachandran had revealed that patients with lesions in the lower temporal lobe of their brain tended to have intense religious experiences, build altars in their homes, and report themselves to be increasingly religious.[18]

It turned out that claims to have found the 'God spot' in the brain reflected a combination of journalistic exuberance and bad neuroscience. Religious experience, it now appears, is the kind of phenomenon that will be more generalized and distributed in the brain, but scientists *have* greatly increased their knowledge of what happens in the brain when religious experiences occur, and even of what causes such experiences. For example, Andrew Newberg and his associates have been able to show that the brain states of experienced religious practitioners during prayer or meditation are distinctly different from the brain states of non-practiced individuals.[19] These studies have since been replicated for Tibetan Buddhist monks, for Franciscan Sisters, and for meditators not belonging to any particular religious tradition. Then, in a remarkable series of studies at Johns Hopkins University in 2006, religiously inclined volunteers were given a synthetic drug with properties very similar to the traditional Native American hallucinogen peyote. The majority of the volunteers had an intense religious experience that they later described as life-transforming. Six months after the event, they still reported the experience as among the three most significant experiences of their lives.[20]

Once again, multiple interpretations of these data are possible. A group of scholars known as 'neurotheologians' argue that even when we limit our theologies to the kinds of conclusions that are consistent with these data, some religiously significant conclusions follow.[21] Newberg and his co-author Eugene d'Aquili, for example, claim that the neuroscientific data point toward an experience of 'Absolute Unitary Being' (AUB), which is accessible to all human beings.[22] Capacity for this experience is universally built into human brains; it proceeds from 'the holistic operator,' and it represents a 'manifestation of religion.' Still, they insist, such experiences do not prove the existence of God or any other particular religious being. Instead, they open us up to a deeper dimension of existence, a kind of holistic mysticism that suggests the unity of all things.[23] If people then form more specific religious beliefs – say, concerning the specific teachings of Mohammed, Jesus, or the Buddha – these represent their own constructions, above and beyond the basic hardwiring toward mystical experience. Such specific religious beliefs are consistent with the neurological findings, but they are not entailed by them.

To strict naturalists, neurotheology, even in this limited sense, is hogwash. Why begin with the scientific study of the brain and then start drawing conclusions about 'Absolute Unitary Being'? Humans evolved large brains based on selection pressures; these brains assist us in adapting effectively to our environment. Human brains produce some strange by-products, such as (occasionally) the experience of timelessness or connection with all that exists. But no metaphysical conclusions should be drawn from such experiences, since they are neurologically well explained without theology.

Not surprisingly, religious thinkers have responded more positively to the data and experiments of the neurotheologians. 'Such experiments do not of course *prove* the existence of God, nor should one expect them to,' they respond.

> But they are fully consistent with theism. If God created human persons (or caused them to evolve), as we believe, we would expect to find ways for them to experience their Creator and sense something of the divine. Science has provided all the evidence it can; we should not be surprised when it reaches its limits.

One begins to realize that this entire debate is not only about the scientific results, the qualities of human persons, or the nature of the divine. It is also about how religious truth claims might be known and tested (if at all), and about the increasingly blurry boundary between the 'natural' and the 'religious.' Here again the debate can make for some rather unusual bedfellows. Scientific conservatives such as Richard Dawkins and religious conservatives set up the question in similar ways – which has led some to describe them as (respectively) 'scientific fundamentalists' and 'religious fundamentalists.' For both groups, religion is only about the *super*natural, about a God who absolutely transcends the world and who works miraculously within it, setting aside natural law at His own discretion. Of course, the scientific atheists think that these miracles never happen, whereas the conservative religious thinkers affirm that they do. Both, however, agree on what religion requires.

For those who do not accept the equation of religion with the supernatural, a very different set of questions arises. For example, could one be a complete naturalist, denying any miraculous activities in the world, and still be religious? Most Buddhists, and an increasing number of religious persons from other traditions, answer with an unhesitating 'Of course!' The Buddha taught the path to Enlightenment, and anyone who wishes can follow the same path. All things are indeed interrelated at the deepest level, but since Buddhism is not a theistic religion, no supernatural dimension needs to be introduced. (Matters are rather more complex in the history of Tibetan Buddhism, or PureLand Buddhism in Japan, where claims are made that would make many scientists rather more uncomfortable.)

What about, say, Judaism or Christianity? Could one practice them without believing in miracles? Could a theist be a religious naturalist? An increasing number of Jews and Christians identify themselves in this way.[24] Almost 50 years ago Thomas Altizer published a Christian theology of the 'death of God,' which he affirmed was fully in the spirit of Christianity; and others have defended similar positions in recent years.[25]

Less radical options are available as well. The physicist and theologian Robert J. Russell has for years defended a 'non-interventionist' understanding of divine action: God really (objectively) acts in the world, but without carrying out physical miracles in the traditional sense, since that would involve setting aside natural laws.[26] A movement known as process theology maintains that God offers a 'lure' at every moment in the experience of every agent in the world. Through these lures God seeks to persuade agents toward the good, yet God never acts coercively to directly bring about miraculous results that would rob finite agents of their freedom.[27] In fact, one can hold to a fairly traditional understanding of God and still deny that God acts miraculously in the world. Even the great Catholic theologian Thomas Aquinas agreed that God could bring about results which remain consistent with natural law.

Christians and Muslims face some particular challenges in this debate. Muslims are expected to believe that the Qur'an contains miraculous prophecies and that the very existence of the Qur'an is itself a miracle. Traditional Christian faith is built around a miraculous event, namely God's raising of Jesus from the dead on the third day after his crucifixion. 'If Christ has not been raised,' St. Paul wrote, 'we are of all men most to be pitied' (1 Corinthians 15: 17–19). Christian thinkers have been involved in conceiving of this resurrection in ways that reduce or eliminate the conflict with natural science.[28] But these remain challenging matters that members of other traditions do not have to wrestle with in the same way.

What conclusions should one draw from this exploration? Wherever one comes down on the various specific debates, it is undeniable that recent work in the neurosciences has led to a far more complex understanding of the human person. Scientists are still working to develop theories that are broad enough to account for the experiences and actions that people carry out in the world. But they have made incredible progress at giving neurological accounts of psychological experience and dispositions. As a result, religious persons today find themselves confronted with an explosion of knowledge in neurology. The human mind or soul, which once appeared to be the exclusive domain of religion, is now being re-explained in increasingly powerful terms by empirical science.

It is too early to say what will be the final result. Will science falsify religious claims about the human person – or at least show them to be so permanently undetectable that they become decreasingly credible? Or will scientific progress leave the core religious questions untouched, so that traditional theological answers remain plausible? Or, finally, will the neurosciences be able to work in partnership with the world's religious traditions to shed more light on what the human person ultimately is? We happen to live in a time when the rhetoric of opposition makes such partnerships difficult. Nevertheless, there are in fact many areas in which scientific and religious views of the human person overlap. There are good reasons to believe that the two groups could work in a complementary fashion to develop more comprehensive and adequate theories of human nature.

QUESTIONS FOR REFLECTION AND DISCUSSION

1. Which theory of mind do you find yourself most attracted to (eliminativist, epiphenomenalist, emergentist, dualist, etc.) and why? What is at stake for you when you answer this question?
2. Consider the different views of mind or consciousness across the various religious traditions. Which religions make very strong claims about mind or soul, and which make the most minimal claims? Which of these views can be most easily synthesized with contemporary neuroscience, and which raise the greatest difficulties?
3. What's the most minimal theory of mind that a religious person could endorse? Can one be religious and a naturalist at the same time? Could one hold an eliminativist view of mind and be religious at the same time? Could one say, 'You're nothing but a pack of neurons' (Francis Crick, *The Astonishing Hypothesis*)?

4. How might the believer in an immortal soul answer the neuroscientist?
5. If religiously significant experiences can be explained neurologically, does this diminish or increase their significance? Try to make the case for the one outcome and then for the other. What might be the implications for religion if neuroscience is able to fully explain other emotions, say, love, guilt, or the desire for justice?

SUGGESTIONS FOR FURTHER READING

Eugene d'Aquili and Andrew Newberg, *The Mystical Mind: Probing the Biology of Religious Experience* (Minneapolis, MN: Fortress Press, 1999).

Eugene d'Aquili and Andrew Newberg, *Why God Won't Go Away: Brain Science and the Biology of Belief* (New York: Ballantine Books, 2001).

Colin Blakemore and Susan Greenfield, eds, *Mindwaves: Thoughts on Intelligence, Identity, and Consciousness* (Oxford; New York: Blackwell, 1987).

Warren Brown, Nancey Murphy *et al.*, eds, *Whatever Happened to the Soul? Scientific and Theological Portraits of Human Nature* (Minneapolis: Fortress Press, 1998).

Patricia S. Churchland and Terrence J. Sejnowski, *The Computational Brain* (Cambridge, MA: MIT Press, 1992).

Paul M. Churchland, *A Neurocomputational Perspective: The Nature of Mind and the Structure of Science* (Cambridge, MA: MIT Press, 1989).

Philip Clayton, *Mind and Emergence: From Quantum to Consciousness* (Oxford: Oxford University Press, 2004).

Philip Clayton and Paul Davies, eds, *The Reemergence of Emergence* (Oxford: Oxford University Press, 2006).

Philip Clayton and Steven Knapp, *The Predicament of Belief: Science, Philosophy, Faith* (Oxford: Oxford University Press, 2011).

John B. Cobb, Jr. and Christopher Ives, eds, *The Emptying God: A Buddhist–Jewish–Christian Conversation* (Maryknoll, NY: Orbis Books, 1990).

Francis Crick, *The Astonishing Hypothesis: The Scientific Search for the Soul* (New York: Scribner, 1994).

Daniel Dennett, *Brainstorms: Philosophical Essays on Mind and Psychology* (Montgomery, VT: Bradford Books, 1978).

Daniel C. Dennett, *Consciousness Explained* (Boston, MA: MIT Press, 1992).

Daniel Dennett, *Elbow Room: The Varieties of Free Will Worth Wanting* (Cambridge, MA: MIT Press, 1984), 75.

Willem B. Drees, *Religion, Science, and Naturalism* (Cambridge; New York: Cambridge University Press, 1996).

Susan Greenfield, *The Private Life of the Brain: Emotions, Consciousness, and the Secret of the Self* (New York: John Wiley & Sons, 2000).

David Griffin, ed., *Deep Religious Pluralism* (Louisville, KT: Westminster John Knox Press, 2005).

David Griffin, *Reenchantment without Supernaturalism* (Ithaca, NY: Cornell University Press, 2001).

John Holland, *Emergence: From Chaos to Order* (Reading, MA: Addison-Wesley, 1998).

Jaegwon Kim, *Mind in the Physical World* (Princeton, NJ: Princeton University Press, 2000).

Benjamin Libet, *Mind Time: The Temporal Factor in Consciousness* (Cambridge, MA; London: Harvard University Press, 2005).

Patrick McNamara, ed., *Where God and Science Meet: How Brain and Evolutionary Studies Alter Our Understanding of Religion* (Westport, CT: Praeger Publishers, 2006).

J. P. Moreland and Scott Rae, *Body and Soul: Human Nature and the Crisis in Ethics* (Downers Grove, IL: InterVarsity Press, 2000).

Andrew B. Newberg, *Principles of Neurotheology* (Farnham, England; Burlington, VT: Ashgate, 2010).

Wesley J. Wildman, *Religious and Spiritual Experiences: A Spiritually Evocative Naturalist Interpretation* (Cambridge; New York: Cambridge University Press, 2011).

Wesley J. Wildman, *Science and Religious Anthropology: A Spiritually Evocative Naturalist Interpretation of Human Life* (Farnham, England; Burlington, VT: Ashgate, 2009).

7

SCIENCE, TECHNOLOGY, AND ETHICS
RESEARCH

By this point some readers will be tired of all these questions about what is true and what is not true, what can be known and what cannot be known. Some will long since have concluded that science is the only reliable guide to knowledge and will be impatient with religious claims and religious reasons. Others will feel just as strongly that 'the heart has its reasons that Reason knows not of' (Pascal). Others may have become agnostic, or just exhausted, in light of the complex and apparently unresolvable debates between scientists and religious traditions.

For such persons this chapter will come, I hope, as a welcome relief. Even if one is highly skeptical of integrating religious *truth claims* with scientific results and methods, religions may still be useful in guiding *ethical* decisions. Perhaps they can serve as repositories of wisdom that humans have acquired over the centuries; or they can motivate people to think less of themselves and more of others and the environment; or, at the very least, they can provide some inspiring examples and helpful aphorisms. While religion cannot necessarily be reduced to ethics, most religious traditions place a major stress on ethical reflection and guidance.

As we will see, science continually raises extremely knotty ethical dilemmas – sometimes in the process of doing scientific research, and sometimes in the questions about what to do with the results. (We focus on research-related issues in this chapter and on issues of application in Chapter 8.) In each case, knowing something about the science is essential for understanding the dilemmas and how they arise. But in almost every case, knowing the science is not *sufficient* for resolving the questions. Philosophers can help in analyzing the dilemmas, finding common features between them, and formulating ethical or meta–ethical theories. But at the end of the day, philosophy has to rely on ethical intuitions and assumptions that have their sources in other realms. Many people find that religious traditions offer complex and often rich repositories of moral and ethical values. One does not need to take the religions as infallible in order to use them as resources for some of the new and difficult dilemmas that science is raising. In fact, even someone who did not hold *any* religious beliefs could find herself in agreement with some of these values.

Obviously, two short chapters cannot cover all the ethical questions raised by science today. I have selected some of the more intriguing, provocative, and urgent among science's ethical dilemmas. In each case, you will find multiple options from among which you can choose. For each issue covered, see if you can identify the response that you think is the most justified. Put together the best case you can make for your answer (your hypothesis). Then see how your arguments fare in discussions with advocates of the other views.

STEM CELL RESEARCH

In human beings the sperm and egg combine to form a single-celled fetus, a zygote. Soon the cell divides into two cells, then four, then eight, and so on, up to the approximately 50 to 75 trillion cells that constitute the adult human body. The new genome that is created by the genetic material from a particular egg and sperm provides instructions for the early 'stem' cells to take on more specific functions. The stem cells gradually become the neurons, bones, and diverse organs of that complex system that is the human body. We call them stem cells because they have the potential to form into any of a large number of specific cell types.

In recent years the great medical importance of these stem cells has been recognized. In a process known as nuclear transfer, the nucleus of the stem cell can be removed and replaced by the nucleus of a specific cell, let us say a pancreatic cell from a healthy person's pancreas. Through cell division, a healthy group of pancreatic cells can then be formed in a short period of time. These cells can then be embedded into the pancreas of a diabetic person, where they continue to reproduce. A vast number of therapeutic uses of this stem cell procedure are currently being developed. Many scientists expect that they will eventually bring life-saving relief for victims of heart disease, brain disease, diabetes, backbone disease, and even cancer.

The trouble is that our major (and, until recently, our only) source of stem cells is fertilized human embryos. In one sense, this is not a problem: contemporary techniques in assisted reproduction, techniques practiced in most fertility clinics, produce large numbers of fertilized eggs, and many of these are kept and frozen at the request of the couples who receive fertility treatments. They are ideal sources of stem cells. In many cases, written permission has already been given for the fertilized eggs to be used for medical research. In this sense, no legal or technical obstacles stand in the way of using the stem cells for medical research and treatment.

But is there a compelling *moral* reason not to do so? Many religious persons have argued that there is. For example, the Roman Catholic view is that God adds the soul to the egg at the moment of fertilization. If the embryo has a soul, it is a living individual in its own right. Metaphysically speaking, it is just as much a person, and hence just as worthy of protection, as any other adult individual. Christian evangelicals have tended to take the same position, appealing to a literal reading of biblical assertions such as, 'You knit me together in my mother's womb' (Psalm 139, NRSV). Indeed, it is not only Christians who believe that persons have souls. Jains affirm that every living thing has a *jiva* or soul, just as Hindus affirm the *Ātman* in each living thing.

The different religious traditions respond in very different ways to the debate about using stem cells. The Jewish traditions – not only Reform and Conservative, but also Orthodox – are much more open to medical experimentation of this sort. Jewish families are threatened by specific genetic diseases such as Tay-Sachs disease. In addition, given the decline in the number of Jewish children being born, it is a matter of religious concern when a Jewish couple wishes to produce children and cannot do so. The official position of Orthodox rabbis in Israel is that medical experimentation is allowed on embryos up to 40 days after fertilization. Rabbis may disagree on the latest point at which experimentation would be acceptable, which would also be the point at which abortion is not religiously allowed. One traditional answer is that this point is reached when the heart begins to beat, but that point comes far, far later than the early stage at which stem cells are obtained. For Muslims, likewise, harvesting and using stem cells is ethically permissible. Some Muslim scholars argue that the limit is 30 days after fertilization, and others 60 days. Since 14 days is sufficient for scientific practice, no conflict arises here either.

If one steps back from the specific positions, three broad families of religious views emerge. The first group maintains that God has already imparted an immortal soul to the fertilized egg, so that it deserves the same protection as any other human being. Similarly, if the embryo becomes a full human being at some precise point in fetal development – when the heart beats, say, or when brain activity begins – then there will be an equally precise dividing line. The second group holds that personhood gradually develops over the course of the pregnancy. Rather than personhood being achieved suddenly (say, by imparting a soul), personhood is a set of capacities that are not present at fertilization. (These views are more similar to the 'gradualism' presupposed in the famous *Roe* vs. *Wade* decision of the U.S. Supreme Court in 1973.)

The exact point at which the process ends is a matter of debate. Traditionally, it was said to be the moment of birth that brought the baby into the full community of human personhood. Increasingly, medical technology has tended to move that point back. Many people feel that, once a fetus is able to survive outside the womb, it should receive legal protection, even if the mother does not wish to carry the baby to term. Given current medical technology, this point of 'viability' can now be as early as 26 weeks, and perhaps even earlier. (Interestingly, some indigenous religions hold that, even after birth, the newborn is not yet a person. It remains in a sort of limbo state until certain religious rituals are performed, such as circumcision or a naming ceremony with the family or village elders.)

A third and final group of religious positions approaches the question with the goal of bringing about a net decrease in suffering. Choosing an early-term abortion, they argue, falls under a woman's reproductive rights. A late-term abortion (say, to save the life of the woman) is a more tragic matter but still causes the least net suffering. On this view, medical research that has the clear potential to save thousands of lives, such as stem cell therapies, should be endorsed on religious grounds, since they are consistent with the call to compassion.

In fact, a number of religious traditions hold that the contribution of religion lies not in setting parameters for the beginning or ending of life, but rather in reducing the overall amount of suffering in the world. In a movement known as 'Engaged Buddhism' in Asia, and in much of Buddhism as practiced in the West, this is the central tenet, traceable back to the Buddha's saying that one should 'cause no harm' (*ahimsa*). Similar principles may be found in Reform Judaism and in 'progressive' forms of Christian theology. Such approaches often view religion as the ally of scientific medicine, at least to the extent that doctors aim to reduce suffering. Still, the religious approval of medical practice is not unconditional. When medicine is practiced for the gain of the researcher and not for the good of patients, for example, or when animals are sacrificed unnecessarily (say, when computer modeling would suffice to produce similar results), then these religious thinkers are not hesitant to criticize scientific practice.

ETHICAL ISSUES AT THE END OF LIFE

The case of Terri Schiavo gained international attention in March, 2005. She was medically diagnosed as being in a 'persistent vegetative state' (PVS). Brain scans showed extreme atrophy in the prefrontal cortex, although some lower brain stem activity could still be detected. Like many such patients, she had been kept alive by means of a ventilator and feeding tube. Neurologist Ronald Cranford concluded, 'beyond any doubt whatsoever Terri is in a vegetative state.'

The case was then catapulted to national prominence by a dispute between her husband, who wanted to remove the feeding tube, and her parents, staunch Catholics, who held that this was equivalent to murder. The ethicist Jack Freer described the dilemma: 'When [the family] sees a warm body and a beating heart, neurological explanations about brainstem function are often not persuasive.' Thus Schiavo's father held that 'She's alive and she's fighting like hell to live, and she's begging for help. She's still communicating, still responding.'

Note that many of the same issues arise here as arose in the case of stem cell research. The official Catholic and conservative Protestant position was that, as long as Terri Schiavo was alive, she had a soul and should thus be treated like any other living person. But this view clashed with the medical view: when the brain has atrophied to this degree, conscious experience no longer occurs. Terri could not be consciously trying to communicate with her family or doctors.

So which side was right? Or is there some third, intermediate position between them? And how does one define death anyway? This last question turns out to be a lot harder than you would think. For example, the fact that a person can no longer eat or breathe on her own is no longer sufficient to define death. In the past, such persons would die quickly. But intubating patients and putting them on a respirator is now common medical practice, and a patient can be held in a persistent vegetative state for many years.

Following medical advice, legislators have tended to define death as 'brain death.' When the brain has atrophied or the EEG is flat, this is a medically irreversible state. Although it is possible still to keep the body breathing, many doctors will say 'there is no point in ventilating a corpse.' All the functions that we associate with living human persons depend on activity in the prefrontal cortex. When that activity has ceased, doctors say, there is no longer any point to 'heroic' measures. After consultation with the family, the feeding tube is removed and bodily functions will gradually end. Note that Pope John Paul II endorsed the position of Pope Pius XII, who said that it is 'for the doctor to give a clear and precise definition of death and of the moment of death.'

But three other religious priorities can make matters more complicated. One is the religious concern with the *quality* of life. 'Cause no suffering!' is merely one side of the coin; the positive side is to maximize the good for all creatures. When it comes to old age, final sickness, and the dying process, religious writings support both the healing function of the doctors and the care-giving function of the nurses. Palliative care, for example – the care given to patients to maximize their comfort and minimize their suffering during the dying process – arguably lies at the center of religious concern.

Another traditional religious priority has been to challenge individualism and to understand persons as always existing within a moral or religious community. This means that religions may urge that decisions about treatment be shared by the broader family, especially in cases where the patient is no longer able to make the decisions herself. When the suffering has reduced the quality of life below a certain minimum, the patient or her family may advocate allowing the disease to run its course, without further medical interventions ('passive euthanasia'). More controversially, some have argued that the patient should be allowed to take steps to hasten her own death, including the ingestion of a lethal substance that will directly end her life ('active euthanasia'). Those who defend active euthanasia often agree that the doctor should not be asked to carry out this function. Over the past few years, several high-visibility cases have caught the attention of the British public, such as the 2009 case of the famous conductor who accompanied his wife to Switzerland and chose to die with her when she elected for a program of active euthanasia.[1]

The final complicating factor is the religious argument for preserving the dignity of the person even when he or she is no longer able to interact personally within the human community. Thus religious persons have worked to ensure that Alzheimer's patients are treated with full human dignity, even when they are no longer able to recognize or respond to the persons around them. Sometimes the ground given is that they continue to possess an eternal soul. Thus a Hindu doctor who worked with Alzheimer's patients once told me, 'I knew that her soul was still alive and intact inside her. So I could not treat her as just a body; I knew that, deep inside, she was still the same person she had always been.'[2] Others make the dignity argument without appealing to the existence of a soul. Human moral community and love should still be extended, they maintain, even to the 'unlovable' and to those who can no longer reciprocate as persons. It is fair to say that, at least from Florence Nightingale on, religious persons have done much to humanize medicine and to decrease the depersonalization that can so easily be the by-product of the medical establishment today.

Given the tendency of the debate about euthanasia to deteriorate into a combat between its most avid defenders and its most extreme opponents, it seems important to close by including a few of the mediating positions. 'Progressive' Jews, Christians, and Muslims tend to focus on more holistic considerations:

I look for the miraculous in the entire process by which life emerges from nonlife, not in individual miracles at each moment of conception. Similarly, I believe the qualities of personhood – what religious people call 'the image of God' – emerge slowly during the months leading up to and following birth.[3]

Religious humanists also bring deep concerns about values to the debate:

The humanist response is more subtle, amorphous and hence harder to describe. But for many nonreligious people, the sense remains that life is somehow sacred even if it is not grounded in a divine creative act. Something more emerges in life, and something more is lost when it ends, than medicine can ever fathom. Perhaps the value of an individual's life is a product of how we treat him or her.[4]

The media sometimes give the impression that, when it comes to the complex decisions about medical treatment at the end of life, one is forced to choose between one of the extreme positions. In fact, however, the real-life questions that families face today very often fall into the 'gray' realm between the black and white options. The more one understands the whole range of factors that impinge on life-and-death decisions, the better equipped one will be to face the reality of the medical decisions that he or she may someday be required to make on behalf of a loved one.

THE RIGHTS OF SUBJECTS IN SCIENTIFIC EXPERIMENTS

What are the rights of human subjects in scientific or medical experiments? It may be tempting to be completely utilitarian about this question. If the suffering of one or a few human subjects can lead to cures that save tens of thousands of lives, that suffering is justified. We know this practice in its most extreme form from the Nazi doctors.[5] When you walk through the museums in the concentration camps Auschwitz and Dachau, you can see photographs of Jewish prisoners being slowly frozen to death in large barrels of water. No more extreme case can be found of eliminating the basic human rights of persons – depersonalizing them – for the sake of the medical knowledge that could thereby be gained.

I should note that these experiments raised an intense ethical debate in the 1980s when the data from the Nazi doctors were rediscovered. Some argued at the time that the data should be used by researchers today in the hopes of decreasing suffering in the future, thereby bringing some good out of the terrible suffering of the Jewish victims of the Nazi doctors. But the overwhelming consensus of doctors, and finally the official position of the American Medical Association, was that the data should not be used since they had been acquired through completely unethical practices.

So what *are* the rights of subjects in experiments? The current standards arose largely out of some controversial cases in the social sciences. In the famous Zimbardo prison experiment at Stanford University, for example, an 'innocent' experiment among volunteers who were role-playing guards and prisoners almost immediately turned brutal.[6] Within a few days of beginning the experiment, the 'guards' became abusive toward their 'prisoners.' The volunteer prisoners were subjected to such intense personal stress in the fake prison that they began to show signs of psychological breakdown. Zimbardo and his colleagues finally concluded that they had lost their scientific objectivity, that they too were being sucked into the pretend world of the prison, so that it was unethical to continue with the experiment.

A similar consensus arose concerning Stanley Milgram's experiments to see whether subjects playing the role of 'teacher' would knowingly harm the subject playing the role of 'student.'[7] When the experimenter asked the 'teacher' to apply a possibly fatal electric shock to the 'student,' the majority of the subjects were willing to follow the experimenter's orders. Even when the 'student' called out, 'Stop, stop, you're hurting me! I have a heart condition! Please stop!' the 'teacher' continued to administer the electrical punishments. Fortunately, the 'student' was actually another experimenter and no shocks were really being administered. But is it ethical to deceive a subject in this way, to put him in a highly traumatic experimental design, and to request him to carry out actions that *he believes* might lead to the death of another person?

The experiments reported in *The Tearoom Trade*[8] also raised a storm of ethical judgments and led to tough new standards for social scientific research. In the original experiment, sociologists posed as watchmen for illegal homosexual encounters in public bathrooms, which allowed them to study how the encounters were arranged. They then traced the car license numbers of the men who had public sex. At a later date another sociologist visited these men at home on a completely different pretext and administered a 'random' survey to them, meanwhile observing their relationships with their wives and children. The data were then compiled and published, although the men were not identified by name. Is it ethical to be an accomplice to illegal activities and to use deception in order to obtain data?

The examples we have considered above raise serious ethical questions. What are the rights of individuals in scientific experiments? At least in these three cases, the community of social scientists has roundly condemned the researchers' actions. Today scientists are required to obtain informed consent from each subject in their experiments. Every major research university has an Institutional Review Board (IRB), which carefully reviews every proposed experiment to make sure that the rights of the subjects have been observed. Deception is tightly controlled, as are experimental designs that might cause trauma or long-term harm to the subjects. Equally stringent standards hold for medical experiments. In some cases, the result has been that medical or scientific knowledge grows much more slowly, since the experiments that are allowed are less effective in gaining new knowledge.

Almost without exception, the interventions of religious persons, and the writings of religious ethicists, have supported this trend. I know of no major religious author who has argued for the opposite answer, which we might call the utilitarian solution: that obtaining more knowledge more quickly justifies trauma, harm, or extensive deception to the experimental subjects. Religious authors have been major advocates for the principle of 'informed consent,' which is now the standard for all such experiments. In this sense we may say that religious thinkers have mirrored the more general focus on human rights that has moved to the center of legal theory and medical ethics.

WARFARE TECHNOLOGIES

This particular topic would be easy if all humans agreed that certain technologies should never be developed. We could then agree on the *reasons* why these weapons should be forbidden, and then governments would ensure that weapons of that sort would never be constructed. Because the community of nations has *not* agreed on such standards, the ethical questions are far more complicated.

The technologies most often mentioned under this category are atomic, biological, and chemical weapons ('ABC weapons'). We all know the devastating effects that followed the dropping of atomic bombs over the Japanese cities of Hiroshima and Nagasaki by the United States in the summer of 1945. In Hiroshima, around 100,000 people were killed instantly, and another 70,000 eventually died from the after-effects of this massive exposure to radiation.[9] Yet these weapons were far less powerful than the nuclear weapons we now possess. Each warhead on an intercontinental ballistic missile (ICBM) has many times the destructive power of the atomic bomb dropped on Hiroshima; and a single missile can deliver multiple warheads. In addition, remember that the radioactivity continues for many years after a nuclear warhead is exploded, so that pregnancies and infants ten or 15 years after the event may still be exposed to damaging levels of radiation.

Biological warfare involves introducing highly lethal organisms into a population. This may include water-borne bacteria, or air-borne viruses such as the Ebola virus that has killed hundreds in Zaire and the Sudan in the past decade. For example, the biological agents might be introduced surreptitiously into the water system of a major city, be dropped into the atmosphere above the city, or be carried into the city and released. In cases where infected human beings would pass the infection on to others, the effects are potentially devastating. Not only a major city, but even much of the population of a country could be destroyed, and the disease could pass well beyond its borders.

Chemical warfare dates back at least as far as World War I. In that war, mustard gas was released in front of one's own trenches in the hope that breezes would carry the thick yellow gas into the opposing enemy trenches, making the troops incapable of battle.

Soldiers affected by mustard gas would experience irritation to the lungs and eyes, with the damage often lasting well beyond the event.

Mustard gas was primitive compared to the chemical warfare materials available today. The United States dropped 'Agent Orange' on Vietnamese forests during the Vietnam War. Agent Orange is a carcinogenic substance, which both caused immediate suffering on the part of the Vietcong soldiers and produced cancer and death over the longer term. It is estimated that about 400,000 Vietnamese died in the short or long term as a result of side-effects of Agent Orange, and about 500,000 children were born with birth defects. Some claim that American soldiers were also injured from the substance, with many dying or experiencing long-term effects. As with biological weapons, chemical weapons could be injected into the water system of a city or dropped from airplanes.

The United States has not signed any treaties that would forbid it to research, produce, and stockpile ABC weapons. The argument given is that the United States would never be the first one to use such weapons, but that possessing these weapons in large and lethal quantities serves as an effective deterrent to any other nation that might want to use them. Critics counter that human beings have never possessed a weapon that they didn't eventually use. Moreover, there is significant danger that such weapons might fall into the hands of more dangerous persons. If these highly lethal biological and chemical weapons get outside the lab, or if they are stolen and resold, they could be obtained by terrorists who would have no compunctions about actually using them. Critics also warn of the dangers that arise during experimentation, transportation, or storage. Even a small leak could have devastating consequences.

Religious voices are divided on the topic of warfare technologies. Some have argued that money should never be spent to develop ABC warfare technologies. These are indiscriminate killers; they are bound to lead to civilian deaths. Not only would they produce massive casualties wherever used, but the lethal effects would probably spread far beyond 'Ground Zero.' In the case of nuclear radiation and some chemical and biological agents, there are also long-term effects that could render an entire region uninhabitable for a lengthy period of time.

One difficulty in the debate is that the technologies themselves are often neutral with regard to warfare and non-warfare uses. Napalm gas, which burned countless people to death during World War II, was discovered by chemists who were not intending to create a weapon. Laser beams now represent a core scientific technology and have broad usages in civilian applications. But for the Department of Defense in the era of Ronald Reagan's missile defense shield ('Star Wars'), potential military applications served as the major driving force for developing new laser technologies. In many other cases, substances now being developed for possible chemical warfare are merely by-products of more general science that are being adapted for use by the military. Basic science itself does not divide into warfare and non-warfare knowledge, even when the *applications* of science do divide up in this way.

Religious supporters of new military technologies usually focus on pragmatic arguments, that is, on the ends that the ABC weapons are supposed to bring about. Since peace is a good thing – so the argument goes – it is acceptable to develop any weapons that bring about or increase the likelihood of peace. Advocates of this position generally agree that the first use of ABC weapons is unethical and is ruled out by their religious tradition. But, they argue, the possession of such weapons for the purpose of deterring *others* from using them is morally acceptable. Further, from the time of the 'cold war' with the Soviet Union to the present, conservative evangelical Christians in the United States have often argued that Communism is godless and immoral, opposed to everything that Christianity, and thus America, stands for. It is therefore our obligation to fight back against the 'evil empire' in whatever ways we can. During the Reagan and two Bush presidencies (20 of the years between 1980 and 2008), this religious argument was used to justify massive build-ups of military technology.

The religious opponents of ABC weapons are more likely to argue that developing and stockpiling these weapons is 'just wrong,' perhaps by appealing to the pacifism of religious figures such as the Buddha, Jesus, or Mahatma Gandhi. Occasionally, pragmatic arguments are also used, emphasizing, for example, the dangers of theft, leakage, or the public dissemination of knowledge about how to produce these 'weapons of mass destruction.' Given the clear and present danger that ABC weapons will be used on civilian populations, and the devastating effects that will follow, it is rather surprising that one does not hear more religiously motivated arguments against them.

QUESTIONS FOR REFLECTION AND DISCUSSION

1. Formulate your own responses to these four urgent ethical issues (stem cell research, treatment of patients at the end of life (euthanasia), the rights of human subjects in experiments, and warfare technologies). In what ways do your religious or anti-religious views play a role in the way that you answer?

2. Do you find yourself able to give definitive answers to the ethical problems considered in this chapter, or are there for you multiple shades of gray? Name some ethical issues in this discussion to which you would apply general principles, and some others where you would say that the answer depends on the context and persons involved. What makes the difference between these two different kinds of cases?

3. What role should religion play in public ethical debates, such as those surrounding warfare technology or stem cell research? Is it better to separate government and religion when making ethical decisions, or can religion play an important role in national debates about burning ethical issues in these fields? Why should people in 'secular' contexts take religious arguments seriously?

4. How does scientific knowledge affect religious ethics? In the end-of-life debate, for example, to what extent should the results of a brain scan determine how we respond to a person in a coma? Are there any religious ethical commitments that 'trump' scientific data? If so, what are they, and why do they 'trump' in this way?

5. Are there particular values (i.e., the sanctity of life, the rights of individuals, decreasing overall suffering) that rise to the top of the scale of importance for you as you weigh these ethical issues? Are these values grounded by religious commitments? Could they be shared by others irrespective of their religious views, or are they particular to your own tradition?

SUGGESTIONS FOR FURTHER READING

Tom Beauchamp, *Principles of Biomedical Ethics* (New York: Oxford University Press, 2009).

Nigel Biggar and Linda Hogan, eds, *Religious Voices in Public Places* (Oxford: Oxford University Press, 2009).

Jonathan E. Brockopp and Thomas Eich, eds, *Muslim Medical Ethics: From Theory to Practice* (Columbia: University of South Carolina Press, 2008).

Lisa Sowle Cahill, *Theological Bioethics: Participation, Justice, and Change* (Washington, D.C.: Georgetown University Press, 2005).

Bernard Cook, *Women and War* (Santa Barbara, CA: ABC-CLIO, 2006).

G. Elijah Dann, *God and the Public Square* (Lanham, MD: Lexington Books, 2010).

Norman Geisler, *Christian Ethics: Contemporary Issues and Options* (Grand Rapids, MI: Baker Academic, 2010).

Sohail Hashmi and Steven Lee, eds, *Ethics of Weapons of Mass Destruction: Religious and Secular Perspectives* (Cambridge: Cambridge University Press, 2004).

Malcolm Jeeves, ed., *From Cells to Souls – and Beyond: Changing Portraits of Human Nature* (Grand Rapids, MI: Wm. B. Eerdmans, 2004).

Peter Lifton, *The Nazi Doctors: Medical Killing and the Psychology of Genocide* (New York: Basic Books, 1986).

Stanley Milgram, *Obedience to Authority: An Experimental View* (New York: Harper & Row, 1974).

Joseph Runzo and Nancy Martin, *Ethics in the World Religions* (Oxford: Oneworld, 2001).

Adil Shamoo, *Responsible Conduct of Research*, 2nd edn (Oxford: Oxford University Press, 2009).

Spencer S. Stober, *God, Science, and Designer Genes: An Exploration of Emerging Genetic Technologies* (Santa Barbara, CA: Praeger, 2009).

Brent Waters, *This Mortal Flesh: Incarnation and Bioethics* (Grand Rapids, MI: Brazos Press, 2009).

8

SCIENCE, TECHNOLOGY, AND ETHICS
APPLICATIONS

'DESIGNER DRUGS': THE ETHICS OF PHARMACEUTICALS

Those who went to primary or elementary school some years back will remember the 'wild kid' in the classroom. He could never sit still; he was always talking out of turn; he was constantly getting into trouble with the teachers. On the playground he would pick fights with others and, as often as not, he would end up in the principal's or headmaster's office by the end of the day. By high school we heard that he was doing drugs and had had his first brush with the law. Later we would hear that he had dropped out of college (if he went at all) and had never been able to make anything of his career. Possibly he 'fell in with the wrong sort' and ended up in much more serious trouble with the law. Perhaps he is now behind bars.

Increasingly, new pharmaceutical products are beginning to change this pattern – at least for those who have access to them. The first step is to define the condition as a medical condition rather than as a moral shortcoming ('he's just a bad kid') or purely legal issue. Vast numbers of schoolchildren are now diagnosed with some form of 'attention deficit hyperactivity disorder' or ADHD. The introduction of Prozac in 1987 and the prevalence of Ritalin in the 1990s was heralded as hope for hyperactive children and those who had difficulty controlling their impulses. Now they can sit still and learn, develop friendships with other children, and remain 'mainstreamed' in the educational system. Books started appearing with titles such as *Finding Myself Again Through Prozac*, *Prozac as a Way of Life*, and *Why Ritalin Rules*.

Those early drugs are primitive in comparison with what is now available. The use of mood- and behavior-altering drugs on a large scale has provided massive amounts of data on how different brains and bodies respond to different chemicals. This explosion in the science of neuropharmacology has led to a much deeper under-standing of the correlations between particular neurochemical states and particular affective conditions. The old paradigm ('here's a mental illness; fix it!') has been replaced by carefully controlled studies of the correlations between chemicals and conscious states. When children respond positively to new experimental chemicals, it actually allows researchers to recognize and name disorders that were previously unknown. (The more cynical response is that the data are being used by money-driven pharmaceutical companies to invent new disorders for which they can design drugs, so that they can increase their profits.) Recognizing new conditions incentiv-izes the search for new drugs with which they can be treated, and the cycle continues.

Not long ago I spoke with one of the leading American neuro-scientists who works in this area. (I was asked not to use his name in this context, so let us call him Dr. Jones.) In light of develop-ments in neuropharmacology over the past 20 years, Dr. Jones pre-dicted a future of ever more precise and nuanced psychotropic drugs. Finally he began speaking of 'designer drugs,' which would take into account the patient's unique genetic features and could be synthesized to match particular features of his or her brain. Almost every antisocial behavior, he predicted, will be treatable with this new generation of chemicals. 'By the time a child is 12 or 13, we will be able to recognize that his brain is likely to produce psychopathic or sociopathic behaviors. Chemical intervention will make it highly likely that we can prevent this juvenile from ending up in prison by age 18 – which almost certainly would have been the outcome without chemical intervention.'

Unlike some researchers, Dr. Jones did recognize that these new abilities will raise massive ethical questions. When are we justified in intervening? How thoroughly will we allow the chemicals to take charge of this young person? Is his or her consent required for such interventions, or his parents, or merely his doctor? And, more generally, what *are* human persons? What is our conscious life anyway, if it can be so precisely determined and transformed by chemical treatments that are designed to correct the 'imbalances' of a particular brain? Religious authors have accused geneticists of 'playing God' when they contemplate genetic enhancements.[1] But is not taking control of a brain by pharmaceuticals an even more dramatic example of 'playing God' in real time? What are the dangers of misuse? Will parents medicate a future Einstein or Mozart, just because his brain and behavior are out of the norm?

Religious scholars have not thought and written about these new dilemmas in the detail that one would have expected. The standard response is a complete rejection. 'It's just wrong,' one sometimes reads, to use drugs to influence the experience and personality of a child to such a great extent. Unfortunately, one has the impression that these comments throw a blanket judgment over a highly complex set of ethical questions. Indeed, one worries that the reason religious people aren't engaging these questions is that they don't want to confront the facts about what science is now able to do. Perhaps they view the self or soul as a purely spiritual entity, so that what is *really* 'just wrong' for these authors is the growing evidence of how deeply a human personality can be transformed by pharmaceuticals.

Other religious responses are utilitarian; they add up the positive and negative consequences and make judgments accordingly, in ways quite similar to secular utilitarian thinking. If a 15 mg. dose of Focalin, a next-generation successor to Ritalin, can change a child's experience of second grade from failure to success, yet without taking away from who she is, then is it not far better for her to be given the drug? If a dosage makes the child lethargic or antisocial or suicidal, then the dosage should be lowered or the treatment stopped. Such responses are wise, but what is distinctively religious about them? In fact, this is exactly how treatment decisions are often made in dialogues between the physician, the parents, and the child's counselor at school. As the child becomes older, she either outgrows the need for the intervention or takes an increasingly greater role in decisions about her medications. By age 18, she is legally free to decide to discontinue the drug – a precedent that most people find also ethically appropriate.

Perhaps the most interesting (potential) religious contribution concerns what new views of the human person we should now adopt given the amazing developments in drug treatments. The most radical inference to draw – and the one that many find the most frightening – is also the one that some scholars are saying is the most justified conclusion to derive from the scientific data. This is the view that what we used to call the 'I,' the self or subject, was just a 'folk psychological' way of naming the electrochemical processes in the human brain. But traditional folk psychology is being challenged by new scientific knowledge, and eventually (they say) it will be completely transformed. At that point we will see human beings as biochemical systems and will control them accordingly. Of course, one may still *speak of them* as persons and treat them *as if* they had free will and moral responsibility, but science will have taught us that such language is actually a fiction.

Yet is this conclusion accurate? It is true that the newer data undercut the belief that we are purely spiritual entities, or that what happens to our bodies has no effect on our thoughts and feelings. But such strictly spiritual views are not widely held today anyway. Moreover, it didn't take the most recent breakthroughs in neuropharmacology to challenge such a strong 'separationist' viewpoint. Already in the 1960s, the novel *Valley of the Dolls* chronicled the excessive use of drugs and anxiety medications, both legal and illegal, in upper-class Hollywood society. For thousands of years humans have observed the changes in behavior and in their experience of the world caused by ingesting coffee, alcohol, marijuana, peyote, and other natural or synthetic chemical substances.

According to this counter-argument, the increased use of mood- and behavior-altering drugs on children and adults in recent years has hardly reduced the human person to her brain anatomy and the chemicals she ingests. What one observes instead is that an initial neurological tendency, for example, toward depression or ADHD, tends to incline the people in the child's environment to respond differently to him. The child then also has some choice of how he will respond in turn. He can respond aggressively to their reactions to him, or defensively; he can become more intellectual, or compensate through sports, or retreat into the world of video games. His brain disorder, even when combined with the reactions from others, does not *determine* which response he will make, although they influence him.

What we see instead – so the argument continues – is that a new character develops in response to these challenges to the child.

Let us imagine that he engages in denial and withdrawal. Those psychological or character-based tendencies in turn incline those around him to make other sorts of responses. (Note that we are already two or three steps removed from the initial neurological condition.) Their responses then pose another challenge for him; he determines how he will act in response to them; and the cycle continues. Brain chemistry plays an important role in influencing this cycle, but it is just not accurate to say that it is the sole determining factor.

This brief example suggests a *multi-leveled framework in which a number of ethical and religious questions can be raised and perhaps answered.* These include:

- Should the drug be administered in the first place? Has it been adequately tested in clinical trials? What are the side-effects, and is it safe? What are the downsides of treatment (e.g., stigmatization of the recipient, other behavioral changes), and do they outweigh the probable gains? Are there viable alternatives to the drug treatment that might have better long-term effects? For example, would individual counseling, or training in social skills, or greater access to sports and outdoor activities, have the same effects? Is a psychological condition being reduced to a medical diagnosis and treated with drugs just because it is simpler for the parents or cheaper for the insurance company?
- When the decision is made to medicate, the treatment needs to be combined with other resources which help the child take advantage of the opportunities that the treatment gives her. In many cases, the social development of the child lags behind due to the medical (neurological) condition. Now that she can sit still in class for the first time, she may need to receive remedial tutoring or help in building friendships with her peers. For example, neurofeedback has been shown to produce better long-term consequences for children with ADHD when used in conjunction with the newer medications.
- The final goal for most religious ethicists is usually the development of the person as a whole. It is interesting that in many languages the word for salvation and for health or wholeness is the same (as in the Latin *salus* or German *Heil*). Religious ethicists make a distinctive contribution when they focus on the

wholeness or well-being of persons and define this as the highest value.[2] Medical professionals often consider their work done and their obligations met when the 'dysfunction' has been minimized and the child is able to function adequately in his or her social context; but no religious tradition limits its interests to this outcome. Each formulates ideals for a full or complete spiritual existence, ideals that include a far more extensive vision of personal and social wellness. Many consider it the great gift of the religious traditions (at their best) to focus attention beyond overcoming particular deficits and on the overall health and well-being of the child or adult. From a religious perspective, medical or psychological therapies may serve as means, but they are not the end of the process.

So how might religious ideals for 'the person as a whole' serve as guidelines for the use of pharmaceutical treatments? The various traditions offer different ways of defining the stages of psychological, moral, and spiritual development – frameworks that are much broader than purely medical or biological definitions of health. They often include ceremonies and rituals to mark important rites of passage. Theological accounts also imply a different, and perhaps deeper, understanding of what the human person is. That understanding leads in turn to broader and more nuanced ethical guidelines for how a patient should be treated, for how a more adequate educational system might be designed, and for the core principles by which health and wholeness can be measured.

What we have found, then, is not a black-and-white assessment of whether the newest generation of drugs, and those now in the pipeline, should or should not be used on children. In many cases, the new drugs have the potential to be immensely therapeutic for a wide variety of different conditions; but serious deficits arise if the treatment is defined in pharmaceutical terms alone. What we are as human persons is truncated and obscured when drug regimes alone define the process and the desired outcomes. The multi-leveled approach considered in this section offers a means for expanding the notion of what treatment and health involve. Arguably, this is one distinctive feature of religiously based ethics.

COMPUTERS, ETHICS, AND ARTIFICIAL INTELLIGENCE

'Computers are depersonalizing,' she complains.

> Instead of talking with each other, kids nowadays spend their entire lives in front of a computer screen. When you want to talk with them, they're always typing something into their telephones. When I call a business, I get a machine voice answering my questions. It just seems like no one talks face to face any more.

Question: How old is the speaker?

For centuries philosophers have spoken of humanity as *Homo faber*, the animal that makes things. With the advent of the modern age, then the industrial age, then the age of electronics, and now the computer age, the pace of human inventiveness has increased exponentially. But is it really a *qualitative* shift? Eyeglasses are technology; so is a house or a telephone. As soon as users become accustomed to a particular invention, it tends to become invisible to them. For one generation, using a telephone disrupted communication more than aiding it; for the next, email did the same ('I'd rather talk to someone on the telephone than emailing them all the time!'); and for the next, it was texting and facebooking (as in 'I'll fb her'). Is it that technologies are *inherently* depersonalizing, or is it one's familiarity with the technology that makes the difference?

The new computing technologies have raised a host of complex ethical dilemmas. In the early days of 'chat rooms,' for example, there was much debate about 'the rape at LambdaMOO.'[3] A number of online friends were gathered in their chat room, sending real-time messages to each other, when a male character named 'Mr. Bungle' launched a 'voodoo,' a sub-routine that allowed him to take over the identities of other characters. The users watched in horror as their characters began carrying out unwanted sexual actions on the screen (not visually, fortunately; it was the era of text-based rather than image-based chat rooms!). They were powerless as their avatars began servicing other characters and expressing their sexual satisfaction in the most graphic of terms, and all the while '[Mr. Bungle's] distant laughter echoed evilly in the living room with every successive outrage.' 'Mr. Bungle' let his voodoo program keep running until the controllers at Stanford University finally shut it down. The primary victim of the rape – the actual person, that is, not her online character – suffered post-traumatic stress disorder. Ethicists asked: Was this a rape? Could the male user who launched the sub-routine be legally prosecuted?

This is just one of the knotty ethical issues that have been raised by the advent of advanced computer technologies. Since those early days we have found that humans have an incredible ability to exist in online worlds, making them not only virtual but also, in myriad ways, real. Advances in technology make this transference of identity increasingly easier. Millions of people around the world lose themselves in online role-playing, either in single-player games or in massive online communities such as SecondLife.com. All the research shows that what happens online has real effects on the flesh-and-blood people who visit the virtual worlds. Governments understand this as well. China recently threatened to shut down a massively popular online game that allows online characters to steal from their neighbors. The reason? A man had just carried out a theft in his neighborhood very similar to the actions allowed in the game.

Parents are thrilled when educational software so enchants their children that they pour themselves happily into acquiring reading, writing, and mathematical skills. But those same parents are rather more concerned when they watch their children killing hundreds of online characters before dinner, leaving each victim to lie writhing in a pool of blood. Parents worry about access to online games with sometimes highly explicit sexual content – especially when these are multi-user games and the parents are not sure who is animating the other characters and what dark real-life goals might be guiding their online activities.

Religious thinkers echo many of the ethical concerns that I have mentioned so far, but different authors draw remarkably different conclusions. Some warn of the inherent dangers of technology, and advocate careful legal and governmental controls (censorship) on how technology is used and what age groups can access various sites. Others prefer a *laissez-faire* approach, stressing the values of personal choice, market forces, and free access to data as a corner-stone of democracy. Countering the 'technophobes' are the religious 'technophiles,' those who claim that the salvation of humankind may lie in technological advances. To the different kinds of predicted breakthroughs correspond different forms of spirituality: the virtually infinite augmentation of human capacities (Nick Bostrom and the transhumanists); the 'singularity' at which the difference between human and robot is overcome (Ray Kurzweil[4]); and in particular the possibility of overcoming death (Aubrey de Grey[5]), thus ushering in life eternal through the god of technology.

ACCESS TO MEDICAL TECHNOLOGIES

Back in the days when the village doctor would come to your house when you were sick, medical treatment was hardly flawless. One did get private care and the full attention of the doctor when he (usually 'he') was there; and being treated in one's own house and bedroom was certainly not depersonalizing. But the level of medical knowledge was much lower then, and your old doctor may well not have mastered the little medical knowledge that doctors had at that time. He didn't bring much technology with him, but in many cases that didn't matter; there really wasn't that much technology to draw from.

Things have changed massively since those days. Let us take a first look at some of the complexities of the health care debate. It will help to show how subtle are the ethical questions raised by the sciences today. Whatever contribution religious thinkers make, they must be at least as complex as the data and challenges.

The typical family doctor in the United States today is a member of a large practice or a Health Maintenance Organization (HMO). She will usually see dozens of different patients each week. The system only works if she can average less than 30 minutes' contact time per patient, each and every workday. All this has tended to turn the doctor into a prescriber of medical technologies and remedies. She is the gateway to advanced medical technology, including tests, drug treatments, and a wide assortment of specialists who administer cutting-edge treatments in more specialized areas. Blood tests and a wide variety of scans will identify most conditions, and the results then indicate which drugs, therapies, or operations should be prescribed for the condition in question.

Although the over-the-counter cost of the drugs easily jumps to hundreds or even thousands of dollars a year, operations are even more expensive. In addition, the large HMOs are able to negotiate significantly lower prices with the major pharmaceutical firms because their doctors prescribe the drugs in such large quantities. Once a certain amount of time has passed, generic versions of these drugs may be produced, and prices drop significantly, but newer pharmaceutical breakthroughs usually mean medications that are sold for very high prices. Uninsured patients with average incomes have little chance of obtaining them, even if their need for the drugs is great. Costs skyrocket when more advanced treatment is needed, and they continue to rise almost exponentially as one moves from outpatient treatment, to operations requiring hospitalization, to critical or life-saving care.

The astronomical costs of medical technology today raise very serious ethical concerns. The trouble is that in this case many of the dilemmas arise directly from the financial realities. For this reason, the debate is often seen as 'merely economic' rather than as involving deeply ethical issues. (It is also true that many of these issues strike closer to home than do other science-and-ethics topics.) Consider these features of the financing of contemporary medicine in the West:

- Some money can be saved through increased efficiency. This includes savings from large HMOs and from increasingly larger groups of physicians practicing together. Technology and computerization have produced cost savings, as has the sharing of information via the internet. Reforms in nationalized health care – in Britain, in Canada, and on the European Continent – have led to further savings, although Americans have so far resisted major reforms. Still, the amount of savings to be expected from bureaucratic reforms is limited; the fact is that contemporary medical technologies are just extremely expensive.
- Part of the cost may be attributed to the fact that many of the players in researching, manufacturing, and delivering medical technologies are for-profit businesses. It is well known that the profits of the large pharmaceutical companies have sometimes been exorbitant.[6] It is also true that the costs of developing new drugs are very high; that there are significant risks that the

research will fail or the drug will not be approved by the U.S. Food and Drug Administration (FDA); and that there is a serious threat of fines and litigation, including multi-million-dollar law-suits. The public is also aware of the take-home pay of medical specialists, especially those who are successful at very difficult or novel surgeries.

- Still, the skyrocketing costs of medical care cannot all be attrib-uted to excesses. Many are systemic. For example, expensive parts made by one company may be assembled into complex machinery by another company. A third company may do the marketing and a fourth the distribution of medical devices to hospitals, which are owned by a (fifth) holding firm or company. Just as oranges, picked by migrant workers for just pennies apiece and sold by growers for small amounts of money, are much more expensive when you buy them in the supermarket because of all the 'middlemen' in between, so also the long 'food chain' in the development, production, and delivery of medical prod-ucts greatly increases the cost for the 'consumers,' the patients.

- The trouble is, these products have to be paid for. Patients can pay for them individually, or HMOs and insurance companies can collect premiums from a large number of people and thereby spread the risk (after deducting money for profits and overheads), or governments can pay for the medical services. With taxpayer resistance mounting and more and more governments forced into strict austerity measures, it is unlikely that governments will run national health programs at a large deficit to themselves over many years. On *each* of these three models, then, the costs for treatment will ultimately be borne by the patients. And yet there is a limit to what patients are able to pay in their monthly premi-ums, as the widespread protests against rising health costs prove only too clearly.

How then can health care costs be held back or 'contained'? The answer is simple, although the ethical and moral issues it raises are not: *not all available medical technologies can be used on all persons who might benefit from them.* In some cases it is the very wealthy who are able to purchase treatment. More often, researchers engaged in a particular program of research choose candidates for experimental treatments or medical trials who are most helpful for research purposes. Of course, these decisions are not always made objectively; sometimes the wishes of the researchers for a particular result, or financial pressures from the organizations that are sponsoring the research, sway decisions about participants.

The more urgent ethical question, however, is raised by this undeniable fact: not all who would benefit from a treatment can obtain it. These decisions are most difficult when it comes to treatments that are out of clinical trials and officially approved. The National Health Service in Great Britain and many nationalized programs on the Continent were among the first to begin making the painful decisions. Kidney or bone marrow transplants will be covered for patients who are young and otherwise healthy enough, but they are not available to patients over a certain age. This policy has led to the fear that patients who are over the maximum age but otherwise healthy may not receive life-saving treatments. Is it ever ethical not to pay for medical care that could extend a person's life? Or, given limited medical funding, is it inevitable that some people will not receive all the technological interventions that medicine could possibly provide?

Although political rhetoric does not treat it this way, this is a genuine dilemma: one is forced to choose between the two poles, even though there are strong arguments on both sides. Here is the argument for the defense: it is simply financially impossible to offer all available treatments to all persons who need them. (In fact, at this time we are still providing treatments to more people than our societies can pay for; more on this in a moment.) Yet holding down costs means that some people who want specialized care will not receive it. The fairest way to limit costs, it would seem, is to formulate general standards or criteria for who receives the available treatments, so that the HMO or national health program only pays for the operation when the person qualifies. But there is an obvious objection: even when the criteria seem fair in principle, there will always be individual cases where we feel that the results are unjust. In addition, if it is one's own mother or father or grandparent or friend who is denied funding for life-saving treatment, one is likely to conclude that the policies are callous, unscrupulous, and unfair.

A central aspect of human nature – an aspect with deep biological roots – is to care more about and do more for those people who are closest to us, and to be rather less concerned about those we don't know. Perhaps this fact explains why the American public seems to show little concern for inequities in access to health care. Some time ago a study showed that there was one physician available for every seven citizens in the wealthy city of Beverly Hills, California, whereas there was about one physician for 2,000 people in poorer areas of the U.S. such as the Appalachian region. Partly these inequities are explained by the economics of the regions in question; partly they are explained by physicians' preference as to where they practice; and partly they are explained by the policies of HMOs and governmental organizations. Access to medical care is a complex social reality; it is too simplistic just to conclude that the wealthier citizens pay more for their medical treatment and therefore get better care. The system as a whole does not operate on a balanced budget; overall, the amount of money spent on patients is higher than the amount paid by the patients. The apparent injustice is that the overspending on the medical needs of much of the American population is made possible by underspending on the medical needs of poorer Americans.

How might the religious traditions assist in answering these medical dilemmas? Sometimes religious voices are raised in defense of the infinite value of each human soul. Throughout the history of medicine, this religious concern has served to block or reduce the 'instrumentalization' of patients. It has served as a reminder of the core principle of the Hippocratic Oath: that the doctor's duty is at all times to work for the good of the patients and to save lives. As the Oath says, 'In purity and according to divine law will I carry out my life and my art.'[7] Thus religious persons have played a major role, for example, in overturning laws that required doctors to carry out executions, say, by administering a lethal injection. Religious groups have also argued against doctors playing a role in 'active euthanasia' (see Chapter 7).

But religious insistence on the infinite value of each human being has also had some more ambiguous results. For example, when those demands result in the policy that 'no cost should be spared' in treating patients, the costs have to be made up from some other source. Sometimes the result is deficit government spending; sometimes it is bankruptcy for physicians' practices or hospitals or HMOs; and sometimes it is inequality in health care provision across the society as a whole. As we saw, when 'the infinite value of each individual' becomes medical policy, money is funneled toward the more demanding segments of the society and away from the poor and other groups who cannot speak up for their own basic needs.

The conflict, in short, is between the 'infinite value' claim and the financial realities of providing health care in the midst of exploding medical costs. Technically, one would need almost infinite resources to pay for treating patients if each one is considered to be of infinite value. Since there obviously are *not* infinite resources, all viable health care systems limit the amount of money they will pay for their clients on an aggregate basis.

Here a deeper conflict arises between two sharply different approaches to religious ethics. The one group (often labeled as 'conservatives') argues for the sanctity of every human life. If a test early in pregnancy shows that a woman is carrying a fetus with Down's syndrome, the mother should not abort the baby but should bring it to term, and the medical system should pay for the costs of caring for this child. Insurance should also cover patients in vegetative states, such as Terri Schiavo (Chapter 7), since it is wrong to discontinue life support. The other group (often called 'liberals') argues for equity in health care benefits across the society as a whole. Conservatives tend to argue for privatized health care programs, so that they can influence the treatment of those closest to them. Liberals tend to argue for socialized health care ('social medicine'), in order that the provision of health care across the entire society will be equitable. The public rhetoric suggests that this is a fight to the death.

Clearly, the short-term recommendations of these two warring factions diverge, sometimes radically; but are the principles that motivate the two groups really incompatible in the end? Not necessarily. One way to test my claim is to ask: could a single individual be motivated by the concerns of both groups and act in conformity with their recommendations, yet without being inconsistent? It appears that she could. Imagine an individual – let us call her Florence – whose religion teaches *both* of the principles in question. Florence watches for cases where *individual patients* are being dehumanized or treated unjustly. Where medical institutions begin to treat an individual patient as a mere machine or statistic,

Florence and her followers come to his aid and lodge complaints. 'Even given the financial limitations on the technologies you can use and the nursing care you can provide,' she insists to the medical staff, 'that doesn't mean that the patient needs to become a mere object in a hospital bed. There are many things you can do to improve her quality of life as a patient within the financial means available to you.' Florence expresses her concern for the value of each patient, but she expresses it in the context of the limited financial resources available.

At the same time, Florence's organization has a deep concern for equity in medical benefits across society – a concern motivated by the same religious commitments and the same awareness of limitations. 'We realize that all segments of the population will face limitations on the medical treatments that can be made available. This is a situation we cannot change. But,' she continues, 'it is also a core religious conviction for me that *all persons* should have access to basic medical care. When I emphasize the painfully deficient treatment available to poor people in my country, I echo the teaching of the scriptures of my tradition, the priorities of our religious leaders, and the examples of our holy men and women. I recognize that establishing policies that are equitable across our entire society may mean that fewer funds are available to me and my friends. But the heart of my tradition teaches that all people are valuable and that I am to put the interests of others equal with, or even above, my own interests.'

QUESTIONS FOR REFLECTION AND DISCUSSION

1. Whose concerns do you tend to think are more important: those of the so-called liberals or those of the conservatives? What particular religious beliefs might lead a person to side with the one group or with the other? Make the best case you can for the one approach to the debate, and then for the other. Wait until you have done both sides before you state what your own views are.

2. What religious assumptions might lead a person to view these two sets of concerns as incompatible? What religious positions would see them as compatible?

3. Is it disturbing that medications are now available which can so radically change someone's personality? Who is the person really: the person she was before the medications, or the person she becomes after she benefits from them? How should these revolutions in medicine change how we think about ourselves?

4. Do you agree that Florence's position is consistent, or do you find inconsistencies in her position? How might different religious traditions answer this question differently?

5. What broader principles might help an entire nation agree on priorities in health care spending?

SUGGESTIONS FOR FURTHER READING

Sudhir Anand *et al.*, eds, *Public Health, Ethics, and Equity* (Oxford: Oxford University Press, 2004).

Ian Barbour, *Nature, Human Nature, and God* (Minneapolis: Fortress Press, 2002).

Aubrey de Grey, *Ending Aging: The Rejuvenation Breakthroughs That Could Reverse Human Aging in Our Lifetime* (New York: St. Martin's Press, 2007).

Lawrence Diller, *The Last Normal Child: Essays on the Intersection of Kids, Culture, and Psychiatric Drugs* (Westport, CT: Praeger, 2006).

David Healy, *Let Them Eat Prozac: The Unhealthy Relationship Between the Pharmaceutical Industry and Depression* (New York: New York University Press, 2004).

John F. Kilner *et al.*, eds, *Cutting-Edge Bioethics: A Christian Exploration of Technologies and Trends* (Grand Rapids, MI: Eerdmans, 2002).

Ray Kurzweil, *The Singularity is Near: When Humans Transcend Biology* (New York: Penguin Books, 2005).

Ted Peters, *Playing God?: Genetic Determinism and Human Freedom* (New York: Routledge, 2003).

Adriana Petryana *et al.*, eds, *Global Pharmaceuticals: Ethics, Markets, Practices* (Durham, NC: Duke University Press, 2006).

Jennifer Prah Ruger, *Health and Social Justice* (Oxford: Oxford University Press, 2010).

Gerald Winslow and James Walters, eds, *Facing Limits: Ethics and Health Care for the Elderly* (Boulder, CO: Westview Press, 1993).

9

THE FUTURE OF SCIENCE AND RELIGION

SUMMARIZING THE OPTIONS

There was a time when it seemed that religion might just disappear. Throughout the modern period secularism continued to grow. It appeared that the religions of humankind would be superseded by science and left behind as historical artifacts, like Egyptian temples, the Greek gods, and many Christian churches in Northern Europe today. Certainly the hope of a world without religion continues to motivate some thinkers. Richard Dawkins' 'Beyond Belief' movement and advertising campaigns in Britain and Canada have precisely this outcome as their goal.

And yet at present the outcome they strive for appears unlikely. If anything, there has been a resurgence of religious commitment around the world. Any decline in religion in Europe and North America has been more than compensated for by the rapid growth of Pentecostal and charismatic movements in churches around the world. Even non-religious thinkers, such as Jürgen Habermas, one of Germany's leading philosophers, now speak of moving – contrary to their and others' expectations – into a 'post-secular society.'[1]

Religion, then, it appears, is not going away. I take it as obvious that science is not going away either (if only because most people love their electronic toys too much). That means we have to find some way to deal with the relationship between these two great cultural forces. What are the possible outcomes? I consider five; perhaps you will be able to formulate others.

(1) It could be that religion is just evil, so that, no matter how long it stays around, it should be opposed. On this view, religion is

like racism or sexism or abusing children: no matter how inevitable it is, we should oppose it whenever and wherever it arises. Something like this seems to be the position of Christopher Hitchens, who titles his book *God Is Not Great: How Religion Poisons Everything*. Hitchens likes the subtitle so much that he repeats it a few pages into the book:

> Religion has caused innumerable people not just to conduct themselves no better than others, but to award themselves permission to behave in ways that would make a brothel-keeper or an ethnic cleanser raise an eyebrow.... People of faith are in their different ways planning your and my destruction, and the destruction of all the hard-won human attainments that I have touched upon. *Religion poisons everything.*[2]

(2) Or perhaps modern science is just wrong. Perhaps one of the religions actually has the true answer, not only about God or the religious ultimate, but also about how the natural world functions. (It seems clear that not *all* the religions can be right, since they say different things about the ultimate nature of reality.)

(3) The religions (or major movements within them) may evolve in directions that become increasingly hostile to science. The scenario might look something like this. Suppose the liberal, progressive, or 'mainline' groups within Judaism, Christianity, and the other traditions continue to develop an openness to scientific methods and conclusions, as they are currently doing. But imagine that the result – say, an integration of Christianity and modern science – fails to provide that sense of meaningfulness and significance that is the primary function of religion. Imagine that too many people become disillusioned with liberal religion – either because it's too distant from the traditions as traditionally taught and practiced, or because it is not distinct enough from the surrounding secular culture, or because in other ways it fails to hold people's religious interest. (Some commentators are saying that this is already happening in Europe and North America. Scholars of India and Asian cultures sometimes write similar things about the declining credibility of traditional religions in those countries as well.)

If this happens, liberal religion wouldn't just disappear, but it *would* become increasingly marginalized. Modernist or progressive religious people would either move on to some sort of generic spirituality, one decreasingly linked to the historical religions, or they would give up on religious concerns altogether. Both responses actually amount to the same thing; after all, 'spiritual but not religious' means, in practice, post-religious. (As we saw, even the greatest opponents of religion today, such as Richard Dawkins and Daniel Dennett, are happy to say that they are at heart deeply spiritual people.)

Such a shift would leave the conservative and anti-scientific positions as the only significant religious voices in Western society. That outcome would certainly produce a sustained, bitter, warfare-to-the-death between science and religion. Conservative religious people would increasingly pull their children out of public schools where standard science is taught, either home-schooling them or placing them in religious schools, yeshivas, and madrasahs. Such people would vote against public funding for basic science research. In the United States, slashing funding for the National Science Foundation, the National Institutes of Health, and the National Academy of Science would further weaken the place of the United States in the world scientific community, with possibly disastrous effects for the American economy. In response, the rhetoric of scientifically interested people toward religion would become increasingly harsh, and the number of religious people in the sciences would presumably decline.

(4) On a more positive level, one can also imagine establishing a (more or less) permanent truce between these two systems of thought. Imagine that scientists and philosophers of science came to agree that religion is concerned about a separate realm altogether.[3] Let us say they were able to precisely specify the domains in which scientific knowledge can be gained, happily leaving the remaining realms to art, literature, philosophy, and religion. One could even imagine that the chief spokespersons for science in our society would in this case even have positive things to say about the arts and humanities, including religious studies – as long as they remained distinct from the sciences and did not make claims to scientific knowledge.

Then imagine that religious thinkers and practitioners accepted a similar distinction, though in their case for religious reasons. They might argue, 'Religion was never intended to be a science of the natural world. It makes metaphysical claims about the nature of ultimate reality, claims about how the natural universe might have arisen, and claims about its final destiny. Revelations and sacred scriptures are about these matters, and about how we should live in the world and with others in light of these beliefs about ultimate reality. But none of these beliefs needs to conflict with science.'

Attempts to include religious beliefs about creation in science textbooks or science classes would immediately disappear. Religious persons might begin to say, 'You know, my belief in God increases my interest in studying the natural world, and that's why I'm becoming an evolutionary biologist or neuroscientist.' Non-religious scientists would be free to pursue their philosophical interests as well — outside of the lab, of course. You can imagine them saying,

> Some people interpret scientific conclusions from their religious worldview, and others (such as myself) interpret them in a completely naturalistic or atheistic way. We both agree that such interpretations are completely independent of the science itself. Sometimes I like to debate about theism and atheism with religious people, but I recognize that these are philosophical debates. Science will never settle the matter one way or the other.

A religious consensus would gradually emerge that passages in the various scriptures and commentaries — passages that many believers today interpret as scientific and historical claims — are actually better interpreted metaphorically or theologically. Phrases such as 'Hindu science' or 'Islamic science' would cease to be used. Presumably theologians would find their own ways to interpret scientific activity from the standpoint of their religious tradition and texts. But these interpretations would always be offered in such a way that the science itself was left untouched.

Similarly, scientists would become very clear about whether they were reporting actual scientific results, possible scientific results, philosophical interpretations of those results, or religious debates about what those results do or do not imply for the various world religions. Of course, maintaining the truce would require some discipline on the parts of both parties, but it certainly seems possible in principle.

(5) On the other hand, maybe the boundaries won't turn out to be so sharp after all. Let us also assume that, as the years go by, only a small number of religious extremists will want to stand in opposition to well-attested scientific results. Imagine that religiously interested thinkers and scientists increasingly become partners in exploring the intriguing borderlands between their fields.

Philosophers and scientifically informed theologians would be invited to join research groups that explore areas of overlap: the neural correlates of consciousness, the co-evolution of biology and culture, the biological foundations of the evolution of religion, and similar topics. As these interdisciplinary groups bring clarity on the key terms and broader speculative questions, they may even help scientists to formulate testable hypotheses about their areas of research. The philosophers and theologians, for their part, would gain new ideas for their fields as they learn more about scientific methods and practices. The discussions would clarify where there are clear scientific results, where there is potential for results, and where questions arise that empirical science cannot resolve. With these results in hand, the philosophers and theologians could formulate their religious (or non-religious) conclusions and understand their own traditions in new ways.

One need not assume that all religious believers would converge upon a single system of belief (though I suppose one cannot rule out this outcome). But one can imagine that people could come to hold a variety of religious interpretations of the world in ways that are compatible with and respectful of the spirit of science. We return below to a few of the positive results that would accrue from this sort of integration.

How can you make up your mind which of these five outcomes is the most plausible? Is there a sixth possibility that is more likely? More importantly, how can you decide which answer would be the most rational, that is, which would correspond to the actual features of science and religion and to the similarities and differences between them? As I hope the earlier chapters in this book have shown, the greater one's knowledge of the sciences and the religions in question, the further one can get. It takes some serious study and dialogue to come up with informed judgments. Discussion with actual scientists and religious people, especially those whose views are not identical to one's own, plays an essential role.

Yet it is more typical today to fire rhetorical salvos in the direction of the opposing camp. The disadvantage of that strategy is that it makes one unsure whether the other side actually possesses any good arguments for their views, thus leaving the rational person with some uncertainties about whether her own position is the best or only possible answer. The battle model makes it impossible to find out whether any compromises or mediating positions are possible. When you hear each member of a couple saying, 'It's all his fault' or 'It's all her fault,' you generally assume some shortcomings on both sides. The impasse has caused them to dig in and toss all blame toward the other, even though the truth lies somewhere in the middle. One cannot help but suspect that something similar is occurring in the impasses that dominate religion–science discussions in our culture today.

Debates will continue as to which of the five options above is actually the best or most likely outcome. Progress is more likely if the participants have some training in questions of religion and science and understand the various options. The author hopes that those who have worked through this book and its questions will now be in a better position to engage in such debates – whichever positions they finally decide to defend.

MAKING THE CASE FOR PARTNERSHIPS

In closing, let us consider a completely different approach to the question about the future of science and religion. Let us assume for the moment that religion *can* serve some positive functions in society. Indeed, many people are able to agree when religion is performing a positive role, even if they don't agree about the truth claims of the religions in question. If so, a society might be motivated to encourage constructive partnerships with and between the various religions – and to convince religious people themselves also to develop such partnerships. And if that's true, the urgent question becomes: What two-way partnerships might be possible, in principle, between religion and science? Consider (and evaluate) these four:

Values from science, values from religion

It is hard to deny that science teaches and exemplifies some particular values. During World War II the famous philosopher of science Karl Popper argued that science stands on the side of 'the open society' and hence against totalitarianism, Marxism, and (his third nemesis) psychoanalysis.[4] Similarly, Jacob Bronowski derived a number of specific values from the practice of science, including dissent, respect, freedom, tolerance, independence, reason, and justice.[5] The well-known new atheist Sam Harris writes in a similar vein when he argues in *The Moral Landscape* that science provides all the values that one needs.[6]

Many people will argue, however, that some value commitments go beyond what science itself can determine. There are universal philosophical principles such as Kant's categorical imperative: 'Act only according to that maxim whereby you can at the same time will that it should become a universal law' or, in its easier form, we should treat persons as 'ends in themselves and not as means only.' One also finds universal (or virtually universal) religious principles such as the call to compassion – perhaps religion's highest principle – and the Golden Rule, 'Do unto others as you would have them do unto you.'

All this suggests a natural form of partnership. Science provides data about the world, and a correct understanding of the world represents the indispensable starting point for any reliable decision-making. Universal principles of fairness and justice then provide a first (and certainly indispensable) context for decision-making. No specific culture or religion should trump the basic requirement that persons are always ends in themselves and never merely a means for someone else's happiness or success.

Beyond this basic framework, however, various kinds of more specific guidance can be provided by specific traditions, each of which is characterized by its own specific principles and priorities. One does not have to endorse all the truth claims of a given tradition to recognize the specific strengths that it brings to the table. Sometimes there will be strong agreement across traditions; at other times one specific tradition may offer insights and emphases that no other tradition makes in quite the same way.

Consider these examples of distinctive contributions from the various traditions. Buddhists emphasize the interdependence of all things, as well as the importance of 'mindfulness' – presence in, with, and to the moment just as it is and for its own sake. Hindu thought has a beautiful ability to recognize the innate value in all individual living things at the same time that it emphasizes their grounding in a single ultimate source and reality. It encourages religious practices that are satisfying and effective in their own right, at the same time that they point beyond themselves to a fundamental spiritual orientation to the world.

Taoism is a beautiful religion of harmony, balance, and cooperation. For Taoist philosophers, whenever one part of society loses sight of its dependence on other parts and begins to dominate, the balance of the Tao is lost, and one should again seek the middle way. Taoism also offers a deep understanding of right action with the concept of *wu wei* or 'without action.' Great results can be achieved without effort (*wei wu wei*: 'action without action' or 'effortless doing') if one retains the balance of the Tao.

Jewish observance draws attention to the importance of consistent practice in the midst of, or perhaps because of, the complexity and ambiguity of human intentions and attitudes. It also places a strong emphasis on the importance of justice and the contribution that people must make to bringing about justice in the world – not despite their religious convictions but because of them. Jewish thinkers have also emphasized the vast difference between God and human beings, hence the unknowability of God, and hence the importance of humility about whatever are one's own beliefs and convictions.

Christianity lays great stress on the internal religious life. This religion always asks not only, 'What did you do?' but at the same time, 'What was your inner attitude when you did it?' It is also a religion that places great stress on love. Its founder, Jesus, said that the two greatest commandments were, 'Love the Lord your God with all your heart, soul, strength, and mind' and 'Love your neighbor as yourself.'

Islam has emphasized the sovereignty of God and the absolute responsibility of humans before their Maker. The five pillars of Islam set high standards for human devotion to God, reminding the believer constantly that all things come from God and will return to God, so that God really is the final judge and determiner of all that exists and occurs. Yet alongside Islam's high standards for obedience are profound mystical writings of devotion to and even unity with the One and Ultimate.

Nor are the contributions limited to the normal list of the 'world religions.' The indigenous religions are the fundamental ecosystems on which later cultures and complex civilizations have been built. Invariably they teach the close bonds between human beings and their specific environment, as well as the interdependence of humans and other animals. No one should romanticize existence in tribal cultures; their relations to animals were often brutal, since life was a matter of 'eat or be eaten.' Yet the interdependence of humans and other animals was understood in a deeply spiritual way. For example, the hunter might shoot and kill a specific animal, but he would often give thanks to the animal in awareness of his dependence on it. Many groups, such as the First Americans who inhabited the wide prairies of North America, developed sophisticated theologies of the sky god, with remarkable similarities to the Abrahamic traditions. Deep commonalities run through the African tribal religions, most particularly in the notion of *ubuntu*, or the interconnectedness of all life. The Liberian peace activist Leymah Gbowee translates *ubuntu* as 'I am what I am because of who we all are.'

Many today argue that humanism should also be understood as one of the human religions. (Other humanists recoil from the idea of treating humanism as a religion.) It is not a theistic religion, but it places great emphasis on improving human living conditions and educational opportunities and fighting for justice for all.

Finally, one can also appreciate specific beliefs and practices within specific traditions even while greeting other aspects of the tradition with more skepticism. Thus some evangelicals condone the emphasis on the family in Mormon belief and practice, as well as some Mormon political beliefs, even while disagreeing strongly with their theologies. And many of the traditions admire the Jain concern for preserving all life forms and avoiding inflicting suffering in any way.

Knowledge, as feminist authors such as Donna Haraway have argued, is always 'situated.' If so, the Enlightenment ideal – that a few universal principles will guide all human beings in their most intimate ethical decisions – is bankrupt. Instead of proclaiming complete relativism and individualism following the demise of Enlightenment rationalism, however, one can also welcome those traditions of belief and practice that are able to provide a meaningful framework for decisions about life-and-death issues. Can some of the value systems that we have just surveyed, either individually or in conjunction, provide such a framework?

The religious traditions and the scientific method

Religions are often associated more with blind belief than with reasoned reflection, but there are aspects in the various traditions that encourage the pursuit of rational discussion and the scientific study of the world. Fostering these connections would be essential for any partnerships with science.

The Abrahamic traditions begin with the creation story in the Book of Genesis. Here humans are given the task of naming the animals and tending and cultivating the earth. This mandate requires that humans *understand* the world – not only as a creation of God, but also in its own right, as an objective reality and hence an object of study and knowledge. The world has value as a creation of God, and believers acknowledge that reality by knowing and understanding its principles and laws. Pursuing scientific knowledge is a natural outgrowth of this responsibility. Historically, this theological justification played an important role in the birth and growth of modern science.

The same shared texts of the Hebrew Bible emphasize that God can be known in and through the natural order, which provides yet another theological basis for studying and knowing the world. Each religion nuances that mandate somewhat differently. The Jewish tradition has emphasized the tasks of studying and gaining knowledge. The call to study began with the Torah and commentary, but it gradually generalized to a major emphasis on studying the world in all its features. In the medieval period, Islamic philosophers played a major role in the development of the new 'natural philosophy,' which eventually gave birth to modern science. There are many Qur'anic texts that stress the order and regularities in the natural world and call Muslims to appreciate and understand that world. Christian theologians developed in particular a strong theology of the image of God (*imago Dei*). In the beginning this concept focused primarily on human beings, but over time it too generalized to recognizing the image of God in all creation.

Other religious traditions were not directly implicated in the founding of modern Western science, but they also gave rise to traditions of study. We have already seen how early traditions of medicine were developed by Hindu thinkers (*Aryuveda*) and Taoist practitioners (traditional Chinese medicine, including herbal remedies and acupuncture). Indian philosophers developed advanced mathematics, Egyptian and Chinese philosophers developed predictive astronomy, and tribal religions developed a deep understanding of the natural rhythms of nature and of animals, including migratory patterns.

Throughout the modern scientific period, religious authors have written theologies that support the pursuit of science and the scientific method – contributions that have often gone unnoticed by scientists and the broader public. In an age when scientific conclusions and the value of science itself are being challenged in many cultures, the religious supporters of science represent important allies. By seeking them out and forming collaborations for the public understanding of science, scientists could do much to deepen the reception of their work within these religious communities.

Compassion and justice

The simplest thing that we associate with religion may also be, in the end, its most valuable contribution. Critics of religion point out the hypocrisy of people who say they serve the God of peace, unity, and love while at the same time they treat their opponents, members of other religions, and even their co-religionists in such unloving ways. Note that the criticism itself acknowledges how deeply rooted is the call to compassion in most of the religious traditions.

Think of the ways in which this call to compassion could have positive effects in the various applications of science and technology. It is true that there are strong market forces to maximize profits. Short cuts on safety contributed to the Union Carbide release of toxic gases in Bhopal, India, in 1984, which killed over 2,200 people and (according to one government estimate) injured more than half a million people, and the massive release of oil by British Petroleum in the Gulf of Mexico in 2010, which produced the world's worst natural oil spill. It is also true that there are political pressures to develop military responses in the face of what one country perceives as threats to its security from another – violent responses that one would hardly describe as compassionate. And it is true, finally, that financial pressures lead hospitals to reduce nursing care, doctors to increase their case loads, technology firms to outsource customer assistance to other countries, and pharmaceutical companies to rush into marketing before thorough clinical testing has been completed.

In each of these cases, informed and knowledgeable religious persons can play an important role. Imagine religious persons working constructively in the various systems and in dialogue with scientific, medical, and business leaders. Of course, to be taken seriously they have to understand how scientific research works and how technology is implemented, including the pressures that operate on these industries and their leaders. When informed individuals then make the call to compassion out of the heart of their particular religious traditions, their voices can be remarkably effective. Imagine these voices spread across society, speaking effectively to many of the different areas where pragmatism and the profit motive tend to drown out all other concerns. If this happened, religious people would surely have the capacity to be a positive social force and to have a balancing effect across the various sectors of society.

Similar partnership is possible in the pursuit of justice. Imagine that representatives of the major religions were to agree in their condemnation of the unjust treatment of individuals, races, or genders. Imagine that it became one of their major roles in society to call nations back to the message of justice that is contained in the founding documents, such as the Magna Carta or the Declaration of Independence.

Non-religious people will rightly respond that it is not the task of the religious traditions alone to exercise compassion or call for justice. One does not have to believe in God to think that it is good to act in a loving manner toward one's fellow citizens or the people in one's neighborhood. This is surely true; religions don't have a corner on the compassion market. Still, non-religious groups that work to mitigate suffering or to bring about more equitable treatment for the disadvantaged will welcome religious groups who wish to become their allies in this endeavor. Surely such involvement is a step up from religious groups that seem only interested in protecting their own rights or debating the sexual habits of their clergy.

Some will dismiss these as idealistic speculations. I admit that there is some justification for their skeptical response; whether religions can really carry out these positive functions in society remains to be seen. Still, recall that in this section we are envisioning what positive relations between science and religion might look like in principle. Surely it cannot be misguided to imagine that religious groups might function to call attention to the values that are basic to their own traditions! And in many of the religious traditions, the call to compassion and justice lies right at the center of their scriptures and founding documents. The individuals whom they venerate as saints and mahatmas ('great souls'), as gurus and enlightened ones, as great rabbis and bodhisattvas, as prophets and reformers, are those who stand for and live by these core principles. If we imagine partnerships in the future where both science and religion are as great as they can be, should we not put compassionate action and the call to justice right at the center of the stage?

The environmental crisis

We close with perhaps the most important example of all. There is overwhelmingly strong scientific evidence that human activities, such as the release of greenhouse gases, are fundamentally changing weather patterns on this planet. People in Europe and North America are only beginning to notice the shifts, but the effects are already striking the global South. Unfortunately, given the nature of the systems in question (for example, the way in which glaciers and ice sheets melt), the impact will be felt gradually at first and then more and more dramatically. Current models suggest that the effects of a continuing increase in greenhouse gas emissions, especially if it moves toward 600 parts per million, will have catastrophic effects on the global environment. The models suggest that the effects of these changes could last as long as 1,000 years.

Scientists have voiced immense frustration that governments and citizens are not responding rationally to the urgency of these data. By and large, the data are being ignored. Worse, members of the public (and some religious groups) have been inclined to challenge the science, offering counter-arguments that are uninformed or, in some cases, patently false. Scientists often ask, 'What more can we do to motivate people to pay more attention to the scientific evidence and to act in ways that will avoid, or at least mitigate, the disaster?'

The partnership of religion with science in this particular area may be their most important joint effort of all. First, note that here – unlike some other topics we have covered in this book – there is a natural division of labor. Religions are not in the position to predict the melting rate of the polar ice caps or to calculate how many meters the sea level will rise as a consequence. Only scientific models can work out the precise consequences for the planet of different levels of greenhouse gases being released into the atmosphere.

By contrast, scientists are, frankly, not particularly good at motivating ordinary citizens to change their lifestyles. Science can explain empirical relationships and causes, but reciting the facts often leaves people cold (as those who work with data know only too well!). Yet science's weakness is precisely religion's strength. For centuries, religions have played crucial roles in influencing their followers' beliefs about right and wrong and in motivating them to live differently in the world. That is what religions do. Religious leaders know how to speak to 'the whole person,' how to motivate not just the head but also the emotions and the will. They know how to construct arguments that appeal to people's most fundamental values and concerns. (The theologian Paul Tillich has even *defined* religion as whatever is of ultimate concern to a person.) There is thus a more natural division of labor here than in perhaps any other area of the science–religion partnership.

Recall that the importance of the natural world and humanity's responsibility to care for it lies right at the heart of many of the world's traditions. The three Abrahamic faiths go back, as we saw, to the Book of Genesis, which calls believers to cultivate and care for the earth. For Jews, Christians, and Muslims, nature is not a lifeless or mechanical thing, a mere compilation of 'matter in motion,' but a creation of God and therefore a thing of great value. As a result, believers in God have every motivation to protect it from destruction, especially destruction at their own hands. Indeed, the doctrine of sin provides a way of conceiving what it means *not* to carry out this responsibility!

The Eastern religious traditions are, if anything, even more oriented to treat the surrounding world as a thing of value. Earlier we studied the call to compassion in Buddhism. In this tradition there can be no temptation to treat the surrounding world as a mere means to human ends, since Buddhists do not single out human beings as intrinsically more valuable than other animals. The central Buddhist call is a call to compassion for *all living things*. A Buddhist environmental ethic is thus central to the entire Buddhist lifeway.

Buddhists have also warmly embraced environmental science and ecology. They argue that it is consistent with the Buddhist teaching of the interdependence of all living things, and that focusing on the welfare of ecosystems – and all the living beings within them – mirrors core Buddhist convictions and practices. Earlier I mentioned the movement known as Engaged Buddhism, which practices ecological activism based on traditional Buddhist principles. For example, Buddhist monks in Thailand have gone into forests that were marked for logging and have conducted the ceremonies of blessing there, placing the mark of blessing on the trees. No Buddhist logger, or anyone who respects the sanctity of the Buddhist practices, could cut down such trees in good conscience, since this is the mark normally placed on a person when she is blessed by the monks. Activist efforts such as these are fascinating, because they bring the resources of environmental studies and the concern with ecosystems together with very traditional Buddhist beliefs and practices.

We also observed that Hindus and Jains recognize a soul in all living things. The process of reincarnation for them not only includes human beings but the *Ātman* or *jiva* of all living things. Thus caring for the earth and preserving the environments on which other living things depend remains at the center of these traditions. This holds even more for the African, Native American, and other indigenous religious traditions. Tribal peoples knew themselves to exist in an intimate balance of receiving and giving with the animals and environment around them. Much more than in contemporary culture, they knew their precarious dependence on the weather and how devastating climate abnormalities such as droughts and floods could be for their peoples.

I saw this partnership in action at the World Parliament of Religions five-year meeting in Melbourne, Australia, in December, 2009. The thousands and thousands of religious leaders from around the world who convened for this summit meeting had chosen climate change and climate justice as one of their core themes. I had the privilege of organizing three large sessions on 'Science, Spirituality, and the Global Climate Crisis' at this event. The Nobel Laureate Peter Doherty opened the first session by listing what we know from science about the causes of climate change and the likely results if current trends are continued. Then panels of religious leaders and scholars from around the world described the grounds within their traditions for treating ecosystems as sacred and for engaging in radical action on behalf of the environment. The sense of shared partnership and common cause was palpable; I had never before heard such a powerful cumulative case for environmental justice. Nor was I the only one; you could see in the faces of the hundreds of religious leaders who were in the audience that they were powerfully influenced by this combination of scientific facts and religious motivations.

Although all the partnerships envisioned in this section are important, the one considered above may be the most urgent of all. Even if all the other collaborations fall through, even if religions and sciences continue to clash over beliefs and worldviews, a successful partnership in staving off a centuries-long climate catastrophe would be enough to make the entire effort worthwhile.

THEY'RE YOUR QUESTIONS NOW...

In the Preface we considered some of the different interests that might draw one into discussions of science and religion. They were divided into three general groups:

1 Religion:

- Religious persons who want to show that their religious beliefs are consistent with today's science.
- Religious persons who have concluded that their beliefs clash with science and who therefore want to be able to convince people that they should side with religion and against science.

- Religious persons who conclude that their beliefs clash with science and who don't want to make affirmations that undercut science, but who are instead trying to determine what (if anything) they can salvage from their religious traditions.

2 Science:

- Scientists who believe that religion is deeply destructive to the quest for scientific knowledge and who want to learn enough about religion that they can demolish it more effectively.
- Scientifically inclined persons who want to find out whether religion is an opponent to science, a friend, or neutral to the scientific quest.
- Scientists who are also religious and who are therefore encouraged by the many compatibilities between scientific knowledge and their religious faith.

3 Other:

- Those who are neither scientists nor religious but who think *both* are important social forces in today's world. These persons want to study the debate to find out whether there is an intrinsic conflict between these two powerful agents in the contemporary world, with the goal of making up their minds about what they should believe and do.
- Those who are interested in the topic for purely intellectual reasons; people who find that it raises some fascinating philosophical questions and who like to reflect and debate about these issues.
- Those who believe that the battle between science and religion is unnecessary, even harmful, and who wish to find ways to decrease the antagonism between the two camps.
- Those who believe there are potential partnerships between science and religion and who want to find ways in which the two might work together more productively.

This impression of a plurality of interests was only intensified as we worked our way through the major debates in the field. We found members of religious traditions who were ready to scrap contemporary science as a whole and to offer their own versions of science in its place. We observed scientists who, perhaps in response, argue the complete incompatibility of science and religion. They want nothing less than for religion to disappear altogether. In most of the topics that we examined, we found these two groups locked in their battle to the death, arguing for diametrically opposed positions on each topic.

As we delved more deeply into the issues, however, we found more and more reasons to wonder whether matters can really be reduced to a single either/or decision. The range of religious beliefs and attitudes turned out to be much broader than one might have expected. Not only are the different religious traditions concerned about very different sorts of issues, but their attitudes toward scientific knowledge vary just as widely. Nor is science a single monolithic theory. The different sciences study vastly different sorts of phenomena, from quarks to kangaroos to consciousness, with each bringing its own set of theories, methods, and types of data. These differences are a part of the story, alongside the common features of scientific method shared across the natural sciences.

Perhaps the fundamental choice the reader has to make is the choice between the incompatibilists and the compatibilists. If one sides with the incompatibility of science and religion, one needs only decide which of the two opposing sides to join. Subsequent decisions become rather simpler. Whenever a new topic comes up – stem cell research or the origins of life or medical ethics – one only needs to know which answer supports his side and undercuts the other side. All the rest are details.

Compatibilists have a somewhat more complex task on our hands, since our view does not lend itself to blanket judgments. For each new debate we need to learn the details of the topic. We need to know which aspects of fundamental science are involved, and which parts of which religious traditions are engaged in the debate. Sometimes we recognize that *these particular religious beliefs* are in tension with *this particular science*. If it turns out that the scientific results are solid, then the religious tradition will have to adapt – perhaps by revising or discarding some traditional beliefs, perhaps by treating those beliefs as mythical or metaphorical, or perhaps in any of a myriad other ways. Often, however, we recognize that the religious beliefs and the scientific results are compatible, perhaps even complementary. It becomes our task to show how and why one can affirm both without having to make an ultimate choice between them.

Like many philosophical questions, the questions that arise at the boundaries between the sciences and the religions are likely to be with us for as long as science and religion continue to exist. For those who love deep and perplexing questions, they offer some of the most complex examples one could hope to find. Here the wonder and the inquiring spirit that draws people into science (and that fuels many of the great scientific discoveries) come together with the awe and wonder that religious people often talk about. Here, surely, is enough material for several lifetimes of reading, dialogue, and reflection.

But the challenge of science and religion also has something to offer those who are less drawn to the speculative questions. One can be a skeptic about the truth questions and yet an enthusiastic supporter of their practical importance. People who are more practically oriented may still believe that the sorts of partnerships outlined in this chapter are potentially of great significance for humanity and this planet.

Especially with regard to the global climate crisis, one should acknowledge the 'opportunity cost' of failing to work together. Those who follow science and take its conclusions seriously know that there are potentially catastrophic consequences for not changing current human patterns of consumption. We are amazed to find people willing to set aside the consensus of scientific opinion or to ignore it (it is not clear which of these two is worse) and to continue current practices at the personal, communal, and national level. One does not have to be religious to welcome any positive role that the world's religious traditions can play in helping to resolve this global crisis. It would be tragic if unnecessary feuding between the scientific and religious establishments meant that the chance was lost for them to work together as powerful allies to affect human policies. That is one opportunity cost we cannot afford to pay.

QUESTIONS FOR REFLECTION AND DISCUSSION

1. Which of the five possibilities for the future of science and religion listed in this chapter seems most likely to you? Which do you think would be most rational given the characteristics of

science and religion? Which do you think would have the best consequences for our society?

2. Can either science or religion by itself support all the values necessary for human flourishing? If not, does one seem to offer more than the other? Which kinds of values are best derived from religious ways of thinking, and which from scientific?

3. Which of the bullet points on pages 167–168 would you use to describe yourself? Are there multiple categories that apply to you? Has your self-definition changed after reading this book?

4. This book has argued for the basic compatibility of science and religion. Are you convinced? What questions or doubts do you have, if any? Should it be a priority for scientific and religious people to improve the relationship between the two?

SUGGESTIONS FOR FURTHER READING

Ian Barbour, *When Science Meets Religion* (San Francisco, CA: Harper San Francisco, 2000).

Jacob Bronowski, *Science and Human Values*, Rev. edn (New York: Harper & Row, 1975).

Stephen Jay Gould, *Rocks of Ages: Science and Religion in the Fullness of Life* (New York: Ballantine Books, 1999).

Sam Harris, *The Moral Landscape: How Science Can Determine Human Values* (New York: Free Press, 2010).

Christopher Hitchens, *God Is Not Great: How Religion Poisons Everything* (New York: Twelve, 2007).

John Polkinghorne, *Science and the Trinity: The Christian Encounter with Reality* (New Haven, CT: Yale University Press, 2004).

Karl Popper, *The Open Society and Its Enemies*, 2 vols (London: Routledge, 1945).

NOTES

1 THE BASIC QUESTION: SCIENCE *OR* RELIGION, OR SCIENCE *AND* RELIGION?

1. Jacob Bronowski, *Science and Human Values*, Rev. edn (New York: Harper & Row, 1975).

2 THE TWO MOST FAMOUS FOES: INTELLIGENT DESIGN VERSUS THE NEW ATHEISTS

1. Francis Bacon, *Novum Organum*, in *The Works of Francis Bacon*, ed. J. Spedding, R. L. Ellis, and D. D. Heath (London: Longman & Co., 1857–1874), vol. IV (1868), Part I, sections 41ff.

2. John Draper, *A History of the Conflict Between Religion and Science* (New York: D. Appleton & Co., 1875).

3. Andrew Dickson White, *A History of the Warfare of Science with Theology in Christendom* (New York: D. Appleton & Co., 1896), online at http://abob. libs.uga.edu/bobk/whitewtc.html.

4. Phillip E. Johnson, 'Evolution as Dogma: The Establishment of Naturalism,' *First Things* 6 (1990), 15–22, republished in Robert T. Pennock, ed., *Intelligent Design Creationism and its Critics* (Cambridge, MA: MIT Bradford, 2001), 59–76, quote 75.

5. See Robert T. Pennock, *Tower of Babel: The Evidence against the New Creationism* (Cambridge, MA: MIT Bradford, 1999); Barbara Forrest, 'The Wedge at Work: How Intelligent Design Creationism is Wedging its Way into the Cultural and Academic Mainstream,' in Pennock, ed., *Intelligent Design Creationism*, 5–53.

6. William A. Dembski, 'Intelligent Design as a Theory of Information,' *Perspectives on Science and Christian Faith* 49 (1997): 180–190, reprinted in Pennock, ed., *Intelligent Design Creationism*, 553–573. See also Dembski and Michael Ruse, eds, *Debating Design: From Darwin to DNA* (Cambridge: Cambridge University Press, 2004).

7. Michael J. Behe, 'Molecular Machines: Experimental Support for the Design

Inference,' *Cosmic Pursuit* 1 (1998): 27–35, reprinted in Pennock, ed., *Intelligent Design Creationism*, 240–256.

8. Behe, *Darwin's Black Box* (New York: Free Press, 2006), 73.
9. Richard Dawkins, *The God Delusion* (Boston, MA: Houghton Mifflin, 2006), 31. The following references in the text are also to this work unless otherwise noted.
10. Alvin Plantinga, 'The Dawkins Confusion: Naturalism ad absurdum,' *Books and Culture* 13/2 (March/April 2007): 21.
11. See, e.g., the famous Catholic scholar of religion and science, John Haught, in his scathing article 'Amateur Atheists' in the *Christian Century*, February 26, 2008.
12. Dawkins, *River out of Eden: A Darwinian View of Life* (New York: Basic Books, 1995), 33.
13. See John D. Barrow and Frank J. Tipler, *The Anthropic Cosmological Principle* (Oxford: Oxford University Press, 1988). For an enthusiastic defense of 'fine-tuning' as a proof of the existence of God, see Hugh Ross, *The Creator and the Cosmos: How the Greatest Scientific Discoveries of the Century Reveal God*, 3rd expanded edn (Colorado Springs, CO: NavPress, 2001). I do not think that the evidence is quite as unambiguous as Ross claims.
14. Dawkins, *Unweaving the Rainbow: Science, Delusion, and the Appetite for Wonder* (Boston, MA: Houghton Mifflin, 1998), 194.
15. See Clayton, 'Contemporary Philosophical Concepts of Laws of Nature: The Quest for Broad Explanatory Consonance,' in Fraser Watts, ed., *Creation: Probability and Law* (Minneapolis: Fortress, 2008), 37–58; Clayton, *Adventures in the Spirit* (Minneapolis: Fortress Press, 2008), esp. pp. 186–203; Austin Farrer, *Finite and Infinite: A Philosophical Essay* (Westminster [England]: Dacre Press, 1943); John Polkinghorne, *Exploring Reality: The Intertwining of Science and Religion* (New Haven, CT: Yale University Press, 2005).
16. See Chapter 5 below.
17. The example is drawn from William H. Durham, *Coevolution: Genes, Culture, and Human Diversity* (Stanford, CA: Stanford University Press, 1991).
18. Susan McCarthy, *Becoming a Tiger: How Baby Animals Learn to Live in the Wild* (New York: Norton, 2004), 4.
19. See Byrne's work on the interpretation of deceptive behavior in baboons *Papio ursinus*, as reported in Richard Byrne, *The Thinking Ape: Evolutionary Origins of Intelligence* (Oxford: Oxford University Press, 1995).
20. Dawkins, *The Blind Watchmaker* (New York: Norton, 1994), 141.
21. Ibid., 141.
22. Alfred North Whitehead, *Science and the Modern World* (New York: Free Press, 1967), 191–192.

3 SCIENCE AND THE WORLD'S RELIGIONS

1. An excellent overview is Noah J. Efron, *Judaism and Science: A Historical Introduction* (Westport, CT: Greenwood Press, 2007). See also Lenn E. Goodman, *Creation and Evolution* (Abingdon, UK: Routledge, 2010), for a

helpful example. Goodman shows how Jews can affirm the best of evolutionary biology while remaining committed to the normativity of their texts and practices.

2. See Jacob Bronowski, *Science and Human Values* (New York: Messner, 1956).

3. See Daniel Matt, *God and the Big Bang: Discovering Harmony Between Science and Spirituality* (Woodstock, VT: Jewish Lights Publishing, 1996); Joel R. Primack and Nancy Ellen Abrams, *The View from the Center of the Universe: Discovering Our Extraordinary Place in the Cosmos* (New York: Penguin Riverhead, 2006). Joel Primack is a leading astrophysicist and a secular Jew; his approach to integrating science and spirituality is markedly different from Orthodox treatments of the same topics.

4. Carl Feit, 'The Order of Creation and the Emerging God: Evolution and Divine Action in the Natural World,' in Geoffrey Cantor and Marc Swetlitz, eds, *Jewish Tradition and the Challenge of Darwinism* (Chicago, IL: University of Chicago Press, 2006).

5. Cyril Domb and Aryeh Carmell, eds, *Challenge: Torah Views on Science and its Problems* (London: Association of Orthodox Jewish Scientists; New York: Feldheim, 1976).

6. Robert Pollack, *The Faith of Biology and the Biology of Faith: Order, Meaning, and Free Will in Modern Medical Science* (New York: Columbia University Press, 2000).

7. Seyyed Hossein Nasr, 'Islam and Science,' in Philip Clayton, ed., *Oxford Handbook of Religion and Science* (Oxford: Oxford University Press, 2006), 85.

8. Similar sets of concepts can be described in a more moderate or a more strident tone. The writings of the Iranian philosopher and physicist Mehdi Golshani are more moderate in tone, e.g., *Issues in Islam and Science* (Tehran: Institute for Humanities and Cultural Studies, 2004), and *The Holy Qur'an and the Sciences of Nature* (New York: Global Scholarly Publications, 2003).

9. Nasr, p. 73.

10. Nidhal Guessoum, *Islam's Quantum Question: Reconciling Muslim Tradition and Modern Science* (London: I.B. Tauris, 2011).

11. Ibid.

12. Adis Duderija, 'The Interpretational Implications of Progressive Muslims: Qur'an and Sunnah Manhaj in relation to [the] Construction of a Normative Muslimah Representation,' *Journal of Islam and Christian–Muslim Relations*, 19/4 (2008): 409–427. For an online source, see Duderija, 'The Political Dimension of Critical-Progressive Islamic hermeneutics,' www.pol.mq.edu.au/apsa/papers/Refereed%20papers/Duderija%20The%20Political%20Dimension.pdf.

13. Taner Edis, *An Illusion of Harmony: Science and Religion in Islam* (Amherst, NY: Prometheus Books, 2007), 203–204.

14. Richard C. Foltz *et al.*, eds, *Islam and Ecology: A Bestowed Trust* (Cambridge, MA: Harvard University Press, 2003); Saleem H. Ali, *Treasures of the Earth: Need, Greed and a Sustainable Future* (New Haven, CT: Yale University

Press, 2009); İbrahim Özdemir, *The Ethical Dimension of Human Attitude Towards Nature: A Muslim Perspective* (Istanbul: Insan Publications, 2008).

15. Bruno Guiderdoni, 'Are Science and Islam Compatible?,' online at http://science-islam.net/article.php3?id_article=618&lang=en. For an in-depth interview with this French astrophysicist and convert to Islam, see W. Mark Richardson and Gordy Slack, eds, *Faith in Science: Scientists Search for Truth* (New York: Routledge, 2001), 70–86.

16. D. P. Agrawal and Lalit Tiwari, 'Ayurveda: The Traditional Indian Medicine System and its Global Dissemination,' online at www.indianscience.org/essays/t_es_agraw_ayurveda.shtml. The same website, edited by Rajiv Malhotra and Jay Patel, includes a wide variety of articles on the history of Indian science and technology.

17. Sangeetha Menon, ed., *Consciousness, Experience, and Ways of Knowing: Perspectives from Science, Philosophy and the Arts* (Bangalore: National Institute of Advanced Studies, 2006); Pranab Das, ed., *Global Perspectives on Science and Spirituality* (West Conshohocken, PA: Templeton Press, 2009); Makarand Paranjape, ed., *Science, Spirituality and the Modernization of India* (London: Anthem Press, 2009).

18. George Sudarshan, 'One Quest, One Knowledge,' in W. Mark Richardson *et al.*, eds, *Science and the Spiritual Quest: New Essays by Leading Scientists* (London: Routledge, 2002), 252, 251, 250.

19. The single most important resource is B. Alan Wallace, ed., *Buddhism and Science: Breaking New Ground* (New York: Columbia University Press, 2003). Among its many excellent chapters I particularly recommend José Ignacio Cabezón, 'Buddhism and Science: On the Nature of the Dialogue,' 35–70. For a dialogue on physics and Buddhism I recommend Matthieu Ricard and Trinh Xuan Thuan, *The Quantum and the Lotus* (New York: Crown Publishers, 2001).

20. Somewhat more cynical observers have called this a public relations ploy, emphasizing how strict is the adherence to a wide variety of doctrinal claims in the monasteries in Tibet. Certainly it would be mistaken to pretend that Tibetan Buddhism does not include, and in many ways rest upon, a rather specific set of beliefs about ultimate reality, causality, and the details of reincarnations, scriptures, and ethics. Still, whether essentialist or innovative, the attitude that the Dalai Lama reflects has a huge influence on how the traditional beliefs are understood and related to evolving science.

21. See Thich Nhat Hanh, *Interbeing: Fourteen Guidelines for Engaged Buddhism*, 3rd edn (Berkeley, CA: Parallax Press, 1998); *Understanding Our Mind* (Berkeley, CA: Parallax Press, 2006).

22. Matthieu Ricard and Trinh Xuan Thuan, *The Quantum and the Lotus: A Journey to the Frontiers Where Science and Buddhism Meet* (New York: Crown Publishers, 2001); Richard J. Davidson and Anne Harrington, *Visions of Compassion: Western Scientists and Tibetan Buddhists Examine Human Nature* (New York: Oxford University Press, 2001).

23. On Buddhist phenomenology, see Dan Lusthaus, *Buddhist Phenomenology:*

A Philosophical Investigation of Yogācāra Buddhism and the Ch'eng Wei-shih lun (London: RoutledgeCurzon, 2002); Chandra B. Varma, *Buddhist Phenomenology: A Theravāda Perspective* (Delhi: Eastern Book Linkers, 1993). More recently, see Evan Thompson, ed., *The Problem of Consciousness: New Essays in Phenomenological Philosophy of Mind* (Calgary, Alberta: University of Calgary Press, 2003), and Evan Thompson, *Mind in Life: Biology, Phenomenology, and the Sciences of Mind* (Cambridge, MA: Belknap Press of Harvard University Press, 2007).

24. Among many publications, see B. Alan Wallace, *The Taboo of Subjectivity: Toward A New Science of Consciousness* (Oxford: Oxford University Press, 2000). The quotes are from 110 and 179f.

25. Traditional Tibetan Buddhists hold a number of commitments that stand closer to the Hindu concerns and are somewhat harder to reconcile with contemporary science, including belief in reincarnation, karma, the Buddha mind, and the continuing existence of Bodhisattvas.

4 PHYSICS

1. Peter Berger, *The Sacred Canopy: Elements of a Sociological Theory of Religion* (New York: Anchor Books, 1990).

2. Carl Sagan, *Cosmos* (New York: Random House, 1980), 214. It has been calculated that a day of Brahma (a *kalpa*) is 4.32 billion solar years long; see http://conscious-universe.blogspot.com/2007/07/brahmas-dream.html.

3. Popular works are Steven Weinberg, *The First Three Minutes* (New York: Basic Books, 1993), and Stephen Hawking, *A Brief History of Time* (New York: Bantam Books, 1988).

4. Or, as William Wordsworth puts it:

> a sense sublime
> Of something far more deeply interfused,
> Whose dwelling is the light of setting suns,
> And the round ocean and the living air,
> And the blue sky, and in the mind of man;
> A motion and a spirit, that impels
> All thinking things, all objects of all thought,
> And rolls through all things.
> > *Lyrical Ballads*, 'Lines Written a Few Miles Above Tintern Abbey'
> > (London; New York: Longman, 1992)

5. Pierre-Simon Laplace, Introduction to the *Essai philosophique sur les probabilités* of 1814.

6. Robert Laughlin, *A Different Universe: Reinventing Physics from the Bottom Down* (New York: Basic Books, 2005), 74.

7. John D. Barrow and Frank J. Tipler, *The Anthropic Cosmological Principle* (Oxford: Oxford University Press, 1986).

8. See Alex Vilenkin, *Many Worlds in One: The Search for Other Universes* (New York: Hill and Wang, 2006).

9. The famous cosmologist and one-time collaborator with Stephen Hawking,

George Ellis, argued this way in an article in *Nature*. See Ellis, 'Cosmology: The Untestable Multiverse', *Nature* 469 (2011), 294–295.

10. John von Neumann, *Mathematical Foundations of Quantum Mechanics* (Princeton, NJ: Princeton University Press, 1955); Henry P. Stapp, *Mind, Matter and Quantum Mechanics* (New York: Springer, 2009); Henry P. Stapp, *Mindful Universe: Quantum Mechanics and the Participating Observer* (New York: Springer, 2007).

11. Stuart Hameroff and Roger Penrose, 'Orchestrated Reduction of Quantum Coherence in Brain Microtubules: A Model for Consciousness,' in Stuart Hameroff *et al.*, eds, *Toward a Science of Consciousness – The First Tucson Discussions and Debates* (Cambridge, MA: MIT Press, 1996).

12. John Archibald Wheeler with Kenneth Ford, *Geons, Black Holes, and Quantum Foam: A Life in Physics* (New York: Norton, 1998); John Archibald Wheeler, *At Home in the Universe* (New York: American Institute of Physics, 1994); John D. Barrow, Paul C. W. Davies, and Charles L. Harper Jr, eds, *Science and Ultimate Reality: Quantum Theory, Cosmology, and Complexity* (Cambridge: Cambridge University Press, 2004).

13. Philip Hefner, *The Human Factor: Evolution, Culture and Religion* (Minneapolis: Fortress Press, 1993).

14. Fritjof Capra, *The Tao of Physics: An Exploration of the Parallels between Modern Physics and Eastern Mysticism* (Boston, MA: Shambhala, 2000).

15. Carl Friedrich von Weiszäcker, *The World View of Physics*, trans. Marjorie Grene (London: Routledge & Kegan Paul, 1952).

16. Amit Goswami, *The Self-Aware Universe: How Consciousness Creates the Material World* (New York: Putnam's Sons, 1993).

17. See Bernard d'Espagnat, *On Physics and Philosophy* (Princeton, NJ: Princeton University Press, 2006), and *In Search of Reality* (New York: Springer-Verlag, 1993).

5 THE BIOLOGICAL SCIENCES

1. Stanley Miller, 'Production of Amino Acids Under Possible Primitive Earth Conditions,' *Science* 117 (3046): 528.

2. I am influenced in the following account by David Deamer and Gail R. Fleischaker, eds, *Origins of Life: The Central Concepts* (Boston, MA: Jones and Bartlett Publishers, 1994), and by subsequent developments in this research program. For a sample of the way in which origins of life research is discussed in science–religion discussions, see the two-part symposium on 'God and the World of Signs' in *Zygon: Journal of Religion and Science*, vol. 45, issues 2 and 3 (June and September, 2010).

3. See Philip Clayton, *In Quest of Freedom: The Emergence of Spirit in the Natural World* (Göttingen: Vandenhoeck & Ruprecht, 2009), chs 2–3.

4. Richard Dawkins, *The God Delusion* (Boston, MA: Houghton Mifflin, 2008).

5. See S. Nasr, 'Islam and Science,' in Philip Clayton, ed., *The Oxford Handbook of Religion and Science* (Oxford: Oxford University Press, 2006).

6. For an opposing perspective, a Muslim compatibilist, see Nidhal Guessoum,

Islam's Quantum Question: Reconciling Muslim Tradition and Modern Science (London: I. B. Tauris, 2010).

7. Richard Dawkins, *The Selfish Gene* (Oxford: Oxford University Press, 1976), xxi.

8. The first part of the quote is from Dawkins, 11; the second is from the 1989 edition, 20.

9. Alessandro Minelli, *Forms of Becoming: The Evolutionary Biology of Development* (Princeton, NJ: Princeton University Press, 2009); Sean B. Carroll, *Endless Forms Most Beautiful: The New Science of Evo Devo and the Making of the Animal Kingdom* (New York: Norton, 2005); Massimo Pigliucci and Gerd B. Müller, eds, *Evolution: The Extended Synthesis* (Cambridge, MA: MIT Press, 2010); Scott F. Gilbert and David Epel, *Ecological Developmental Biology: Integrating Epigenetics, Medicine, and Evolution* (Sunderland, MA: Sinauer, 2009); J. Scott Turner, *The Tinkerer's Accomplice: How Design Emerges from Life Itself* (Cambridge, MA: Harvard University Press, 2007).

10. See Jesper Hoffmeyer, *Legacy for Living Systems* (New York: Springer, 2010); *Biosemiotics: An Examination into the Signs of Life and the Life of Signs* (Scranton, MI: University of Scranton Press, 2008).

11. Stuart Kauffman, *Investigations* (Oxford: Oxford University Press, 2000) and *At Home in the Universe* (New York: Oxford University Press, 1995).

12. The Chimpanzee Sequencing and Analysis Consortium, 'Initial Sequence of the Chimpanzee Genome and Comparison with the Human Genome,' *Nature* 437 (2005): 69–87.

13. See Michael Tomasello, *Origins of Human Communication* (Cambridge, MA: MIT Press, 2008); Tomasello and Elizabeth Bates, eds, *Language Development: The Essential Readings* (Malden, MA: Blackwell, 2001).

14. Melvin J. Konner, *The Tangled Wing: Biological Constraints on the Human Spirit*, 2nd edn (New York, 2002).

15. Bharati Puri, *Engaged Buddhism: The Dalai Lama's Worldview* (New Delhi: Oxford University Press, 2006); Sallie B. King, *Being Benevolence: The Social Ethics of Engaged Buddhism* (Honolulu: University of Hawaii Press, 2005); Sulak Sivaraksa, *Conflict, Culture, Change: Engaged Buddhism in a Globalizing World* (Boston, MA: Wisdom Publications, 2005).

16. John Grim, 'Native Lifeways,' in Clayton, ed., *The Oxford Handbook of Religion and Science* (Oxford: Oxford University Press, 2006), 88, 89.

17. Grim, 91.

18. Dawkins, *The Selfish Gene*, 3rd edn (Oxford: Oxford University Press, 2006), 201.

6 THE NEUROSCIENCES

1. Francis Crick, *The Astonishing Hypothesis: The Scientific Search for the Soul* (New York: Scribner, 1994), 3f.

2. See Patricia S. Churchland and Terrence J. Sejnowski, *The Computational Brain* (Cambridge, MA: MIT Press, 1992); Paul M. Churchland, *A Neurocomputational Perspective: The Nature of Mind and the Structure of Science* (Cambridge, MA: MIT Press, 1989); Colin Blakemore and Susan Greenfield,

eds, *Mindwaves: Thoughts on Intelligence, Identity, and Consciousness* (Oxford; New York: Blackwell, 1987); Susan Greenfield, *The Private Life of the Brain: Emotions, Consciousness, and the Secret of the Self* (New York: John Wiley & Sons, 2000).

3. See Jaegwon Kim, *Mind in the Physical World* (Princeton, NJ: Princeton University Press, 2000).

4. Daniel Dennett, *Brainstorms: Philosophical Essays on Mind and Psychology* (Montgomery, VT: Bradford Books, 1978), 171.

5. Dennett, *Brainstorms*, 164f.

6. Daniel Dennett, *Elbow Room: The Varieties of Free Will Worth Wanting* (Cambridge, MA: MIT Press, 1984), 75.

7. Benjamin Libet, *Mind Time: The Temporal Factor in Consciousness* (Cambridge, MA; London: Harvard University Press, 2005), 124.

8. Libet, 124.

9. See J. P. Moreland and Scott Rae, *Body and Soul: Human Nature and the Crisis in Ethics* (Downers Grove, IL: InterVarsity Press, 2000).

10. According to the *Catholic Encyclopedia*,

> The traditional philosophy of the Church holds that the rational soul is created at the moment when it is infused into the new organism.... [T]he rational soul is created when the antecedent principles of life have rendered the foetus an appropriate organism for rational life.... [M]ost neo-Scholastics hold that the rational soul is created and infused into the incipient human being at the moment of conception.

11. In John Wisdom, *Philosophy and Psychoanalysis* (Oxford: Blackwell, 1953).

12. See Warren Brown, Nancey Murphy *et al.*, eds, *Whatever Happened to the Soul? Scientific and Theological Portraits of Human Nature* (Minneapolis: Fortress Press, 1998).

13. See the articles by scientists in Philip Clayton and Paul Davies, eds, *The Reemergence of Emergence* (Oxford: Oxford University Press, 2006); John Holland, *Emergence: From Chaos to Order* (Reading, MA: Addison-Wesley, 1998); Harold Morowitz, *The Emergence of Everything: How the World Became Complex* (New York: Oxford University Press, 2002); Philip Clayton, *Mind and Emergence: From Quantum to Consciousness* (Oxford: Oxford University Press, 2004).

14. Daniel C. Dennett, *Consciousness Explained* (Boston, MA: MIT Press, 1992), 107.

15. Daniel Dennett, *Consciousness Explained*.

16. Clayton, 'Contemporary Philosophical Concepts of Laws of Nature: The Quest for Broad Explanatory Consonance,' in Fraser Watts, ed., *Creation: Law and Probability* (Minneapolis: Fortress, 2008), 37–58.

17. Sharon Begley, 'Your Brain on Religion: Mystic Visions or Brain Circuits at Work?,' *Newsweek* (May 7, 2001).

18. V.S. Ramachandran *et al.*, 'The Neural Basis of Religious Experience,' Annual Conference of the Society of Neuroscience, 23 (1997).

19. Although I am not allowed to reproduce the images here, some of them are accessible at http://andrewnewberg.com/research.asp.

20. Roland Griffiths *et al.*, 'Mystical-type Experiences Occasioned by Psilocybin Mediate the Attribution of Personal Meaning and Spiritual Significance 14 Months Later,' *Journal of Psychopharmacology* 22(6) (2008): 621–632, http://csp.org/psilocybin/Hopkins-CSP-Psilocybin2008.pdf.

21. Andrew B. Newberg, *Principles of Neurotheology* (Surrey, England; Burlington, VT: Ashgate, 2010); Patrick McNamara, ed., *Where God and Science Meet: How Brain and Evolutionary Studies Alter Our Understanding of Religion* (Westport, CT: Praeger Publishers, 2006).

22. Eugene G. d'Aquili and Andrew B. Newberg, *The Mystical Mind: Probing the Biology of Religious Experience* (Minneapolis, MN: Fortress Press, 1999); d'Aquili and Newberg, *Why God Won't Go Away: Brain Science and the Biology of Belief* (New York: Ballantine Books, 2001).

23. Andrew Newberg, *Principles of Neurotheology* (Burlington, VT: Ashgate, 2010).

24. Willem B. Drees, *Religion, Science, and Naturalism* (Cambridge; New York: Cambridge University Press, 1996); Wesley J. Wildman, *Science and Religious Anthropology: A Spiritually Evocative Naturalist Interpretation of Human Life* (Farnham, England; Burlington, VT: Ashgate, 2009); Wesley J. Wildman, *Religious and Spiritual Experiences: A Spiritually Evocative Naturalist Interpretation* (Cambridge; New York: Cambridge University Press, 2011).

25. Thomas Altizer, *The Gospel of Christian Atheism* (Philadelphia, PA: Westminster Press, 1966); Mark Taylor, *After God* (Chicago, IL: University of Chicago Press, 2007).

26. See Robert J. Russell, *Cosmology from Alpha to Omega: The Creative Mutual Interaction of Theology and Science* (Minneapolis, MN: Fortress Press, 2008).

27. John B. Cobb Jr. and Christopher Ives, eds, *The Emptying God: A Buddhist–Jewish–Christian Conversation* (Maryknoll, NY: Orbis Books, 1990); David Griffin, *Reenchantment without Supernaturalism* (Ithaca, NY: Cornell University Press, 2001); David Griffin, ed., *Deep Religious Pluralism* (Louisville, Ky.: Westminster John Knox Press, 2005); Lewis Ford, *The Lure of God: A Biblical Background for Process Theism* (Philadelphia, PA: Fortress Press, 1978); and Catherine Keller, *Face of the Deep* (London; New York: Routledge, 2003). Process theologians derive inspiration from the British philosopher Alfred North Whitehead; see in particular *Process and Reality*, corrected edn (New York: Free Press, 1978).

28. Philip Clayton and Steven Knapp, *The Predicament of Belief: Science, Philosophy, Faith* (Oxford: Oxford University Press, 2011).

7 SCIENCE, TECHNOLOGY, AND ETHICS: RESEARCH

1. Matthew Weaver, 'British Conductor Dies with Wife at Assisted Suicide Clinic,' *Guardian News and Media* (July 14, 2009), www.guardian.co.uk/society/2009/jul/14/assisted-suicide-conductor-edward-downes: 'Downes, 85, was almost blind when he and his 74-year-old wife, who had become his full-time carer, travelled to Switzerland to end their lives.' In the UK, 'anyone assisting a person to end their life could face up to 14 years in

prison.' But prosecutors tend not to press charges against families and friends of people who travel outside the UK for physician-assisted suicide.

2. See also similar comments in Stephen Post's beautiful text, *The Moral Challenges of Alzheimer's Disease* (Baltimore, MD: Johns Hopkins University Press, 1995).

3. Philip Clayton, 'A Mystery of Body and Soul,' *Washington Post*, April 3, 2005, p. B01, www.washingtonpost.com/wp-dyn/articles/A20455–2005Apr2.html.

4. Quoted from Clayton, 'A Mystery of Body and Soul.'

5. See Peter Lifton, *The Nazi Doctors: Medical Killing and the Psychology of Genocide* (New York: Basic Books, 1986).

6. Philip G. Zimbardo *et al.*, 'The Mind is a Formidable Jailer: A Pirandellian Prison,' *The New York Times Magazine* (April 8, 1973), Section 6, 36ff.

7. See Stanley Milgram, *Obedience to Authority: An Experimental View* (New York: Harper & Row, 1974).

8. Laud Humphreys, *Tearoom Trade: Impersonal Sex in Public Places* (Chicago, IL: Aldine Publishing, 1970).

9. Bernard Cook, *Women and War* (Santa Barbara, CA: ABC-CLIO, 2006), 283.

8 SCIENCE, TECHNOLOGY, AND ETHICS: APPLICATIONS

1. Ted Peters, *Playing God?: Genetic Determinism and Human Freedom* (New York: Routledge, 2003).

2. Historically, the doctrine of the inalienable rights of the individual person also has its roots in this religious perspective, as in the work of the English Reformation thinker Richard Hooker.

3. See Julian Dibbel, 'A Rape in Cyberspace,' *Village Voice*, December 21, 1993, http://cyber.eserver.org/rape.txt, accessed November 14, 2010.

4. Ray Kurzweil, *The Singularity is Near: When Humans Transcend Biology* (New York: Penguin Books, 2005).

5. Aubrey de Grey, *Ending Aging: The Rejuvenation Breakthroughs That Could Reverse Human Aging in Our Lifetime* (New York: St. Martin's Press, 2007).

6. Sidney Wolfe, '$2.3 Billion Pfizer Settlement is not Enough to Deter Bad Behavior in the Pharmaceutical Industry,' *Public Citizen* (September 2, 2009), www.citizen.org/pressroom/pressroomredirect.cfm?ID=2954, accessed November 22, 2010.

7. 'The Hippocratic Oath,' *National Library of Medicine*, www.nlm.nih.gov/hmd/greek/greek_oath.html, accessed November 22, 2010.

9 THE FUTURE OF SCIENCE AND RELIGION

1. Jürgen Habermas, 'Notes on Post-Secular Society,' *New Perspectives Quarterly* 25(4) (2008): 17–29.

2. Christopher Hitchens, *God Is Not Great: How Religion Poisons Everything* (New York: Twelve, 2007), 6, 13.

3. Stephen Jay Gould took a position like this in *Rocks of Ages: Science and Religion in the Fullness of Life* (New York: Ballantine Books, 1999).

4. Karl Popper, *The Open Society and Its Enemies*, 2 vols (London: Routledge, 1945).

5. Jacob Bronowski, *Science and Human Values*, Rev. edn (New York: Harper & Row, 1975).

6. Sam Harris, *The Moral Landscape: How Science Can Determine Human Values* (New York: Free Press, 2010).

INDEX